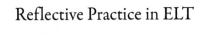

Reflective Practice in ELT

Reflective Practice in Language Education
Series Editor: Thomas S. C. Farrell, Brock University

This series covers different issues related to reflective practice in language education and includes an introductory book which presents an overall discussion of these areas. The other books in the series clarify the different approaches that have been taken within reflective practice and outline current themes that have emerged in the research on various topics and methods of reflection that have occurred.

Forthcoming:

English Language Teacher Beliefs
Farahnaz Faez and Michael Karas

Micro-Reflection on Classroom Communication: A FAB Framework
Hansun Zhang Waring and Sarah Chepkirui Creider

Surviving the Induction Years of Language Teaching: The Importance of Reflective Practice
Thomas S. C. Farrell

The Reflective Cycle of the Teaching Practicum
Fiona Farr and Angela Farrell

Using Video to Support Teacher Reflection and Development
Laura Baecher and Steve Mann

Reflective Practice in ELT

Thomas S. C. Farrell

SHEFFIELD UK   BRISTOL CT

Published by Equinox Publishing Ltd.

UK: Office 415, The Workstation, 15 Paternoster Row, Sheffield,
        South Yorkshire S1 2BX
USA: ISD, 70 Enterprise Drive, Bristol, CT 06010

www.equinoxpub.com

First published 2019

British Library Cataloguing-in-Publication Data
A catalogue record for this book is available from the British Library.

ISBN-13 978 1 78179 653 5 (hardback)
         978 1 78179 654 2 (paperback)
         978 1 78179 655 9 (ePDF)

Library of Congress Cataloging-in-Publication Data
Names: Farrell, Thomas S. C. (Thomas Sylvester Charles), author.
Title: Reflective practice in ELT / Thomas S. C. Farrell.
Description: Bristol, CT : Equinox Publishing Ltd, [2019] | Series:
  Reflective practice in language education | Includes bibliographical
  references and index.
Identifiers: LCCN 2018047852 (print) | LCCN 2019011216 (ebook) | ISBN
  9781781796559 (ePDF) | ISBN 9781781796535 (hb) | ISBN 9781781796542 (pb)
Subjects: LCSH: English language--Study and teaching. | Reflective learning.
Classification: LCC PE1066 (ebook) | LCC PE1066 .F37 2019 (print) | DDC
  428.0071--dc23
LC record available at https://lccn.loc.gov/2018047852

Typeset by S.J.I. Services, New Delhi, India

Contents

Introduction

I have had a long interest in the topic of reflection and reflective practice (RP) related to second language teaching and in particular teaching English to speakers of other languages (TESOL). Over the years I have been lucky to work with many excellent pre-service, novice, and in-service second language teachers worldwide on a wide range of issues and I have learned a great deal from these wonderful professionals about reflection. Interactions with them have substantially contributed to my writings on topics such as novice language teachers' transition in the first year (Farrell, 2016a, 2016d, 2012c, 2008, 2003); the importance of RP in TESOL teacher education programs (Farrell, 2016c, 2012c); international perspectives on ESL teacher education (Farrell, 2015a); expectations and reality during the practicum (Farrell, 2007a); teacher beliefs and role identities (Farrell, 2016e, 2011); competencies and teachers' expertise associated with effective teaching (Farrell, 2015c, 2013c); framework for TESOL professionals (Farrell, 2015b); development groups and collaborative discussions (Farrell, 2013a, 1999); reflective writing (Farrell, 2013b); teaching the four skills (Farrell, 2012b); mapping conceptual change through critical reflection (Farrell, 2009); Dewey and Schön's contributions (Farrell, 2012a); RP in action for busy teachers (Farrell, 2004); RP in both research and practice (Farrell, 2007b), and many more.

These topics and more importantly my interactions with all these teachers have informed and shaped my ideas about reflection and reflective practice and led me at this point in my research to conceptualize a whole series dedicated to RP in language education. This first book, *Reflective Practice in ELT*, introduces the new series for Equinox publishing: **Reflective Practice in Language Education** (https://www.equinoxpub.com/home/reflective-practice-language-education/) that covers different issues related to RP in language education. The other books in the series clarify the different approaches that have been taken within RP and outline current themes that have emerged in the research on various topics and methods of reflection that have occurred. I am of course, honored and delighted to be the editor of this new series and as the terms 'reflection' and 'reflective practice' have become commonplace in many different professions, I believe we should devote more space to spelling out exactly what these terms mean for the field of language education and how reflection and RP can be best utilized by language educators.

Generally then this new series encourages language teachers to develop their own thinking about their practices with the overall aim of being able to provide the best opportunities for their students to learn the language they are teaching. Teachers are encouraged to take the responsibility for their own development through critical reflection on their unique experiences in their particular contexts. They are encouraged to articulate their teaching philosophies, teaching principles, teaching theories, and teaching practices, and critically reflect on the profession they are members of. Such deep reflections enable language teachers to have their voices heard through storytelling, writing, recording, and any such creative means of representing their professional selves so that they become generators of knowledge rather than passive receivers of so-called expert knowledge. Teachers know their own world best, and reflection on that world can make it more accessible to those who work in it – be they teachers, students, administrators, policyholders, or any involved stakeholders.

Reflective Practice in ELT is the first book in the series and as such the chapters provide an overall introduction into the interesting yet complex topic of reflection.

Reflection and reflective practice have now become common terms used in teacher education and development programs worldwide. However, there is still not agreement across the professions about how to define the concept or indeed what strategies promote reflection. Chapter 1 will first discuss the terms reflection, reflective practice, and critical reflection to set the scene for the remainder of the discussion on what RP is. Different definitions of RP as outlined in the literature on general education and TESOL, and the different levels of reflection, are presented here.

Chapter 2 outlines and discusses different typologies of reflective practice starting with John Dewey's original typology and then moving to Donald Schön's development of Dewey's reflective inquiry model. Since Schön's work led to reigniting interest in reflective practice, many different typologies developed and these are discussed in this chapter. They include typologies by David Kolb, Graham Gibbs, Christopher Johns, Stephen Brookfield, and Terry Borton. The chapter also outlines and discusses my own understanding of the concept of RP in the field of TESOL and my interpretation of this concept through my two typologies of reflection: an early typology as well as a relatively new typology or framework for reflecting on practice for TESOL professionals.

Chapter 3 presents six principles of RP. *Principle 1: Reflective Practice is Holistic; Principle 2: Reflective Practice is Evidence-Based; Principle 3: Reflective Practice Involves Dialogue; Principle 4: Reflective Practice Bridges Principles and Practices; Principle 5: Reflective Practice Requires a Disposition to Inquiry; Principle 6: Reflective Practice Is a Way of Life.* These principles show how the important concept of RP is not just a collection of methods to 'fix' perceived problems related to teaching. The six principles outlined and discussed in this chapter point to the depth associated with reflection that starts with the teacher-as-person and extends into and beyond the classroom to encompass a teacher's career and life.

Chapter 4 discusses the reflective tools or instruments most frequently employed by teachers, and how they can be used. These include dialogue, writing, classroom observations, action research, narrative study, lesson study, case analysis, and concept mapping. The chapter also discusses the benefits and challenges for teachers of using such tools as they reflect on their practice.

Chapter 5 describes one experienced TESOL teacher's reflective journey using a framework that included reflections on his philosophy, principles, theory, practice, and beyond practice. The results of his reflective journey revealed that the common themes of approachability, art-oriented conceptions, and curiosity emerged in all aspects of his reflections. However, these themes did not emerge in the same form in each aspect of the teacher's reflections, but rather as uniquely influential parts of a larger whole. The holistic framework for teacher reflection employed in his journey provided multiple filters through which these various parts could be viewed. The complex and dynamic nature of this type of reflection attests to the importance of frequent reflective practice for gaining a complete understanding of the factors that influence what teachers do in the classroom.

Chapter 6 outlines and discusses how reflective practice can be cultivated individually and within a school or institution so that it can move from its customary place in many institutions as a mandatory ritual to a more meaningful developmental and collaborative process for teachers, and for administrators. RP will be more powerful if it is more collegial and if everyone sees its benefits as an integral part of organizational life in such educational settings. The chapter begins though by suggesting that before we can encourage a culture of reflection in a school, we must first cultivate a reflective disposition in individual teachers within the school.

The final chapter poses ten important questions related to reflective practice: 1. Has reflective practice become just another bandwagon? 2. Has TESOL embraced reflective practice? 3. How can we make reflective practice workable for all teachers? 4. Is it possible to teach pre-service language teachers to reflect? 5. Can reflection be faked? 6. Is it possible to assess reflection? 7. Can reflective practice be used for teacher evaluation? 8. What are some of the criticisms of reflective practice?

9. What are the benefits of engaging in reflective practice? 10. What is the future for reflective practice? The chapter attempts to answer each question, but of course some aspects of reflection would be inevitably omitted in my answers. As a result, I am hoping the questions (and my answers) will generate more discussion and reflection on RP.

The primary audience for this book consists of those taking courses in Applied Linguistics/TESOL who are going to become teachers. CELTA, DELTA, and MA TESOL students who study the contents of this book will be better prepared for the realities of what they will face in real classrooms and real schools. I see this book as being a component of all language teacher education programs be they introductory certificate courses or other graduate and post-graduate courses. Pre-service teachers in teacher education programs can use it as a textbook. Program administrators, cooperative teachers, and supervisors who are responsible for training and educating teachers will find the book very useful when it comes to encouraging teachers to reflect, as the research results are overwhelmingly positive and each chapter provides a guide to how teachers (novice and experienced) can implement such reflections. In addition, experienced teachers can use this book as a refresher for their professional development as they look at the various problems of practice that are presented and compare them to their own contexts.

The book is written in a clear and accessible style and assumes no previous background in language teacher education or reflection. Thus introductory courses as well as graduate courses will be able to use the book with ease. Native speaker and non-native speaker language teachers alike will be able to interact with the contents of the book because of its accessible writing style and comprehensible vocabulary. Each chapter has reflective breaks in appropriate places where readers can pause to think about what the research has revealed and where they stand on the particular issue.

As an introduction to the series and the books that are to follow, I hope that *Reflective Practice in ELT* sets the tone and nature of the series and offers a practical introduction to a complex topic. The series will consist of several practice-oriented books that introduce cutting-edge research and practical applications of that research related to reflective practice in language education. I wish all readers happy reflections with this book and the entire series.

Chapter 1

What Is Reflective Practice?

Introduction

Reflection and reflective practice (RP) have now become common terms used in teacher education and development programs worldwide. Miles et al. (1993), for example, surveyed initial teacher education courses in England and Wales and found that over 70% of the courses described some form of reflection, reflective practice, and/or reflective inquiry that was to be included as represented in their program promotions and pamphlets. However, not one of these promotions or pamphlets defined what this reflection was or what it entailed though they all implied that it was a good thing. Indeed, most teacher educators agree that some form of reflection is a desirable practice for all teachers and as Tabachnick & Zeichner (2002: 13) have pointed out, 'there is not a single teacher educator who would say that he or she is not concerned about preparing teachers who are reflective.' Indeed, I believe that no teacher educator would suggest that reflection or engaging in reflective practice is not a good thing, and none would advocate for the unreflective practitioner. Other professions too consider reflective practice as a mark of professional competence and a number of them (e.g., medicine, law, business, nursing, and many more) include the concept of reflection and reflective practice in many of their foundation programs. Thus it is safe to say that RP is seen as a crucial element of education and development programs in most professions including education, and the concept of reflecting in general is advocated by most teacher educators as being an essential skill that needs to be nurtured in all teachers.

Although RP has gained such prominence in several professions worldwide as a mark of professional competence, and is considered a significant component of many foundational education programs and practice within those professions, there is still not agreement across the professions about how to define the concept or indeed what strategies promote reflection. In the field of education most teacher educators, although they agree that reflection is important for teachers, cannot seem to agree on any definition of what reflective practice is and what it entails, and in addition the literature does not provide a mutually agreed upon definition or even an approved model on how RP should be operationalized (Farrell, 2015b, 2018a; Freeman, 2016).

Since its emergence in the field of second language teacher education (SLTE) in the early 1990s, and as a result of developments in the field of general education, RP has also become an almost mandatory term added to most language teacher education and development programs in the field of teaching English to speakers of other languages (TESOL). In addition, within the field of TESOL, RP has arguably become more important in a period of 'post-method condition' where teachers can no longer rely on prescribed teaching methods to get them through lessons (Kumaravadivelu, 2003).

However, as within the field of general education as explained above, the increase in popularity of RP in the field of TESOL has also brought about an array of different definitions and approaches most of which originate from the general education literature (Farrell, 2018a). In a recent review of the research on RP in TESOL, Farrell (2018a) has noted an array of different definitions (if indeed reflection is defined at all), approaches, methods, and typologies that are designed to encourage teachers to reflect on their practice. In some instances Farrell (2018a) has noted that the terms reflection, reflective practice, and critical reflection are used interchangeably indicating that they mean the same thing, but, as the contents of this chapter will outline, they do not all mean the same thing. So although most language educators still agree that some form of reflection is a desirable, the precise definition of RP remains vague with resulting misunderstandings about the philosophical traditions behind whoever's work is cited when attempting to define this interesting, yet complex topic.

This chapter will first deliberate over the terms *reflection*, *reflective practice*, and *critical reflection* in order to set the scene for the remainder of the discussion on what RP is. The chapter then outlines several different definitions of RP as represented in the literature in general education and in TESOL, as well as the different levels of reflection. Chapter 2 will continue to address what RP is by outlining all the different typologies/approaches to reflection. I hope that these two opening chapters will thus provide sufficient information for teachers, researchers, administrators, and interested stakeholders to be able to come to their own conclusions about how they want to define and approach RP for their particular purposes.

Reflective Break

- What is your understanding of the term 'reflection'?
- What is your understanding of the term 'reflective practice'?
- What is your understanding of the term 'critical reflection'?

Sorting Terms: *Reflection, Reflective Practice, Critical Reflection*

'Reflection' can be traced back to ancient times and various religions and of course Socrates' famous quote: 'the unexamined life is not worth living.' The term 'reflection' itself comes from the Latin word 'reflectere' and means 'to bend back' (Valli, 1997: 67) or to look back and become more aware of a past event or issue or to think about it. From ancient historical roots (e.g., ancient Greece, China, and India) it has been recognized that we humans all tend to 'reflect' in some manner in our daily lives, which can be called 'commonsense reflection'. For many people such commonsense reflection in our daily lives involves a process of many different thoughts passing through or even flooding our minds at great speed. As a result, usually these thoughts remain unorganized and we do not tend to link them together in any pattern or even link them to our previous thoughts of that day or the day before, unless we have something 'serious' on our minds. In fact, we are usually self-absorbed when we are engaged in such commonsense reflections and contemplations (this is often represented in idiomatic language as being 'lost in thought') because it is a solitary exercise and we are usually focused only on the self.

Within an educational setting such 'commonsense reflections' can also take place as teachers 'ponder'/'contemplate' about something before going into a class, such as the students' state of mind, or the lesson topic of that particular class, or something else. Teachers can also contemplate immediately after a class and/or while they are on the way home about what occurred during the lesson. These can be called 'commonsense teacher reflections'. Indeed, some may even say that this *is* reflective practice because they 'ponder', 'contemplate', 'think', 'consider', and even 'critically reflect' in such a 'commonsense manner' before, during, and/or after each class. Of course, many teachers report, they are always 'reflecting'.

Herein rests the root cause of some of the vagueness attached to the terms 'reflecting'/'reflection', 'reflective practice', and 'critical reflection' in that they are used interchangeably as meaning the same thing in a catch-all in terms of their focus. For example, what does it mean to 'reflect' before or after class? Does this 'reflection'/'reflecting' include thinking about what happened in terms of behavioral aspects of teaching and learning (a teacher's actions/students' actions) or is this a 'deeper form of reflection' to include the teacher's and students' beliefs about learning and teaching, the teacher's philosophy and theory of teaching, and the deeper social meaning of the act of teaching and its impact on the community outside of the classroom? In addition, how can we be sure that the teacher's (and students') recollections of the events of the lesson are in fact accurate? Is memory reliable and can a teacher or student recall all the events of a lesson? There are many more questions we could ask but the ones posed above are not easy to answer because they involve different theoretical stances towards the concept of 'reflection' and 'reflective practice'. For example, a common question brought up in the literature on reflection and reflective practice is: Should reflection only be conducted on and in classroom actions (behavioral), or should reflection include issues related to education both inside and beyond the classroom, such as social issues?

These particular questions are in fact represented in some of the early definitions of reflection as well. For example, concerning the former stance of focusing reflection on classroom issues exclusively, Cruickshank & Applegate (1981: 553) have suggested that reflection is a process that 'helps[s] teachers to think about what happened [in the classroom], why it happened, and what else could have been done to reach their goals.' This definition positions reflection and RP directly in the classroom in what I call a 'reflective practice bubble' because it also suggests that RP focuses only on problem-solving in a 'fix-it' type of action that the teacher takes. In fact, the teacher-as-person is not involved at all in the reflective process because the reflection focus is retroactive in nature. Thus not all scholars agree that RP should only focus on what occurs in the classroom; they suggest that the process should also include the broader historical, sociopolitical, and moral context of schooling so that reflective teachers can, as Jay & Johnson (2002: 80) maintain, 'come to see themselves as agents of change.' This stance towards reflection and RP sees the teacher as a 'thinking human' who not only provides lessons to students in a classroom (or other places) but also notes the impact of the wider community in which the lessons take place. Jay & Johnson (2002) suggest that as a result of reflecting on practice, teachers should not only attempt to change their own practices, but also those of the outside community and society so that we can live in a more equitable world.

The above different theoretical stances within the field of education have also impacted the field of TESOL and reflective practice. Within TESOL over the past years two main forms of reflection have emerged: a 'weak' form and a 'strong' form. In its weakest version, RP was said to be no more than 'thoughtful' practice where language teachers sometimes, as Wallace (1996: 292) suggested, 'informally evaluate various aspects of their professional expertise.' This would correspond to the 'commonsense reflection' outlined above. According to Wallace (1996:13) this type of 'informal reflection' does not really lead to improved teaching and can even lead to more 'unpleasant emotions without suggesting any way forward.' Indeed, I have found that if teachers are not psychologically ready to reflect on their practice, such reflections can be harmful beyond unpleasant emotions because they can lead to teachers second-guessing what they do all the time, and eventually to what I call 'teaching paralysis' resulting in teachers just following the textbook so as to avoid any upsetting feeling. Wallace (1996) was also alluding to the fact that what we 'think' is happening in our lessons may not 'actually' be happening because we are basing our conclusions solely on our perceptions after the fact and, as noted above, we cannot be sure that we can recall accurately what actually happened in our classes. In such a manner we can become uneasy about the whole notion of reflecting because we are not sure about the accuracy of our reflections.

A second, 'stronger' form or stance toward reflection in language education also emerged and noted that in order to have an accurate recollection of what occurs in lessons teachers need to collect some evidence rather than relying on memory that can in fact be very selective. The 'stronger' form of reflection thus proposed that teachers systematically collect data about their teaching and use the information from that evidence to make informed decisions about their teaching so that they take more responsibility for the actions they take in their classrooms (Farrell, 2007b/2018b). Richards & Lockhard (1994: 1) emphasized this stance and explained it as an approach where teachers 'collect data about their teaching, examine their attitudes, beliefs, assumptions, and teaching practices, and use the information obtained as a basis for critical reflection about teaching.' This stronger stance moves a teacher beyond the fleeting thoughts after a class to gathering specific information (called data) about what actually occurred during the class and making decisions based on the data rather than perceptions of what happened. Walsh & Mann (2015) have since echoed this call for evidence-based RP by encouraging teachers to collect data as a concrete means of focusing reflections so that they can make more insightful analysis and gain a fuller sense of their own teaching.

I too believe that such an evidence-based approach (i.e., data collection) is essential to reflective practice, be it through journal writing, narrative accounts, classroom observations with video and audio evidence, and/or group discussions. Here is a real example from my early work on RP that I still think is important: Imagine a teacher returning home after a day of teaching and 'reflecting' (i.e., pondering) on the day's lessons as having gone well or not so well. The questions that the second stance above would ask are: How do you, the teacher, know the lesson went well, or not so well? What evidence do you, the teacher, have about this perception? Indeed, I realized the importance of such questions many years ago when

I started my first teacher reflection group in Seoul, South Korea in the early 1980s when nobody had heard about reflection or reflective practice in language teaching. A group of teachers (including myself) decided to 'reflect' on our practice for one semester, which included meeting face-to-face once a week as a group to discuss our teaching. One particular week as we were just about to begin our meeting, one of the group members, another teacher at the university I was teaching in, rushed into the meeting room apologizing for being late because her class had just ended. I asked how her class had gone and she had a big, broad smile on her face saying that it went great. Then I asked her how she had reached that conclusion about the lesson. She said she had 'that great feeling' during class and the students 'looked happy' all through the lesson. As her classroom was very near to our meeting room and her students were still visible through the glass doors of the room, I suggested she go ask her students about their opinion of that particular lesson. She did, and she returned fifteen minutes later with her smile gone. She said that her students reported that they may have 'looked happy' during the lesson but this was only because they were about to begin a four-day holiday away from classes and they could not contain their happiness during her lesson. In fact, when she asked her students to recall the events of the lesson and what they had learned, none could. They said sheepishly that they really had not listened to nor understood what she was teaching. The teacher seemed devastated and I felt bad for opening up this 'Pandora's box of teaching'. Later we settled into our group meeting and discussed what we all had observed and this led us as a group to consider what RP actually means to us teachers and how we can and should include our students in the reflective process, given that we had never before considered asking their opinion of our teaching or lessons.

Reflective Break

- Which version of reflective practice do you support: the 'weak' form or the 'strong' form, and why?
- Do you agree with Walsh & Mann's (2015) call for more evidence-based reflective practice by encouraging teachers to collect data about their practice? Why or why not?
- If you agree with the call for teachers to collect data, what kind of data and how much evidence is enough?
- Do you have any similar experiences of watching your students' reactions during your lessons and using those reactions to judge the success or not of your lessons?

From the standpoint of exploring and examining what happens during a lesson, I support the 'stronger' version of collecting evidence about practice rather than having a vague feeling (the commonsense approach?) about what is happening or what has happened, because our perceptions may not be correct and we may be very selective in what we choose to recall about our lessons and take an unduly negative (or sometimes unduly positive) view of what occurs. I have found that teachers can be overly critical about their practice, only recalling what they perceive as negative events during the lessons and forgetting about what went well or the positive events that occurred. Thus they may not be doing themselves or their students justice; in fact, they are actually doing a good job all along but just do not know how to 'look'. So, if teachers want to 'improve' their teaching, which of course many supervisors and administrators think is the *real* purpose of RP, a good start would be to discover what it is they *actually do* in their classrooms, not what they *think* they do. However, in order to discover what they actually do in their lessons, they must systematically gather evidence/data about those lessons and use this to make *informed decisions* about their practice both inside and outside the classroom.

Within the field of TESOL I would suggest that *both* of these contrasting theoretical stances (the weak and strong approaches to reflection) outlined above have taken hold in different ways, and when scholars push the second, stronger stance many also include the term 'critical reflection' to mean teachers considering *why* they do what they do. In other words, the stronger stance that encourages teachers to gather data about their practice to answer the question of *what* they do as well as the question of *why* they do what they do is considered 'critical reflection'. I maintain, however, that this is *not* a correct representation of what the term 'critical reflection' means or is about, and like the terms 'reflection' and 'reflective practice', this term has also not been clearly defined or discussed within the field of general education and TESOL. As Hatton & Smith (1995: 35) have noted, the term 'critical reflection' in the field of general education, 'like reflection itself appears to be used loosely, some taking it to mean more than constructive self-criticism of one's actions with a view to improvement.'

So what does the term 'critical reflection' mean? In order to critically reflect on our practice we must move beyond description of what we do and how we do it, as well as move beyond examining why we do what we do from a theoretical, conceptual level of reflection, to examine the ideological influences behind our practices. In other words, if we take the position that all education is ideological in some manner, then it is better to articulate our particular ideologies and reflect on them to make sure they represent what we really think about our practice within a particular context. Hatton & Smith (1995: 35) go even further and maintain that critical reflection 'implies the acceptance of a particular ideology.' This view of critical reflection also calls for considerations of moral and ethical problems and involves 'making judgments about whether professional activity is equitable, just, and respectful of persons or not' (Hatton & Smith, 1995: 35).

Just as Zeichner & Liston (1996/2014) noted over 20 years ago, the wider socio-historical and politico-cultural contexts can and should also be included in any critical reflection focus. However, this has not been the case within the field of TESOL as the term 'critical reflection' has been used loosely by many TESOL scholars to mean conceptual reflection or to answer the 'why' question of what we do, not the ideological stance that critical reflection really entails. One early notable exception within the field of TESOL is Bartlett (1990) who saw a need to include the broader society in any definition of reflection within language teaching. Bartlett (1990: 204) noted that in order for language teachers to become critically reflective, they must 'transcend the technicalities of teaching and think beyond the need to improve our instructional techniques.' However, I believe that that is as far as we have come in TESOL and nothing has happened to include any real critical reflection in the field up to the present day as publishers and others continue to try to tell language teachers what they 'should' do in their classes. Indeed, the field of TESOL has long suffered from the 'methods obsession' pushed on us by outsiders who are looking to cash in on a young field that is still trying to find its way in choppy academic waters that insist on attempting to keep us down, while at the same time making money off our backs in language institutes (fondly known by many who teach in them as 'cash cows') whose only role on campus is to generate funds to 'real' research. In addition, over the years many publishers have also attempted to take unfair advantage of our clients by pushing glossy textbooks, tapes, CDs, and now computer-generated materials without much input from the teachers who must use them. Indeed, I would go so far as to say that it is time for TESOL as a profession to stand up and become more critically reflective beyond examining what works or does not work in teaching, and examine those who have exploited us over the years and some who continue this exploitation.

Harsh comments, you may say, but in fact, this is real 'critical reflection' on our field. Thus I support Hatton & Smith's (1995: 35) call that the term 'critical' in teaching should include 'making judgments about whether professional activity is equitable, just, and respectful of persons or not' because I believe this focus may offer a useful way forward when defining critical reflective practice within the field of TESOL. I will return to the issue of critical reflection later in the chapter when I outline and discuss different levels of reflection.

Reflective Break

- Are you a critically reflective practitioner? If yes, how do you know and how 'critical' do you think TESOL teachers should become?
- What is your impression of TESOL as a profession?
- Do you think the profession has been exploited by anyone?
- Do you think that my critical reflections on the TESOL profession are unduly harsh?

Towards a Definition

As noted above, it has not been easy to define what reflection or reflective practice is because of the different views about what should be included in the approach and process of reflection. As already discussed, some definitions try to include the broader society as being a major influence while others see reflection as only focusing on what happens in the classroom; yet others still only consider reflection as a commonsense looking back on events in a lesson. In this section I outline and discuss various definitions of reflection as they appear in the literature on both general education and TESOL, with the idea that teachers can test them out in their own contexts and confirm or deny what definition works for them. Eventually they will adopt a definition (and approach) that they are comfortable with or, as Dewey (1910/1933: 209) suggests, 'adopt it as personal knowledge.'

Reflective practice has been in vogue in recent times in the field of general education but it really started with the seminal work of John Dewey in early 20th-century US. At that time Dewey was interested in encouraging more reflection in student learning (rather than with teachers) because he was worried that routine thinking and routine decision-making by students in educational settings would come in the way of a complete education. However, he later spread this idea of reflective inquiry to teachers, noting that teachers who do not bother to reflect on their work become slaves to routine because their actions are guided mostly by impulse, tradition, and/or authority rather than by informed decision-making. This decision-making, Dewey insisted, should be based on systematic and conscious reflections (the 'strong' form of RP outlined above) because he said that teaching experience when combined with these reflections can lead to awareness, development, and growth. Dewey (1910/1933: 9) maintained that such reflection entails 'active, persistent, and careful consideration of any belief or supposed form of knowledge in light of the grounds that support it and the further consequences to which it leads.' This of course has been the most cited definition in the literature and research studies on reflective practice in general education, and has been used by many of the most prominent scholars on RP to indicate their particular definition of reflection. This famous quote in fact has proved to be the basis of many future approaches to reflection and RP, as the concept (re)gained a resurgence in the 1980s with the work of Donald Schön (1983, 1987): his questioning and thinking critically about 'knowing-in-action', and the resultant 'reflection-in-action' when the 'knowing-in-action' is unclear. However, his work with Chris Argyris (Argyris & Schön, 1974, 1978) and their notion of 'double-loop learning' (theories of action) occurring when an error is detected and corrected (as opposed to 'single-loop' learning that remains at the tacit level or deeply entrenched in the individual's subconscious) preceded Schön's (1983) work on practitioner-generated intuitive practice (I return to this work in more detail in chapter 2).

These two wonderful scholars, John Dewey and Donald Schön, have come to be synonymous with the terms reflection and reflective practice throughout the literature and have laid the basis of how many scholars have defined RP in recent times. There was a resurgence of interest in reflection and RP in the 1980s with the press for the empowerment of teachers and the need to find some way to counteract a spike in burnout in the teaching profession and to re-think the notion of the dominant assumptions of technical rationality. This was manifested in professions outside education as Schön (1983) in particular maintained that professionals know more about their practice than they can articulate and thus they can also generate knowledge (through reflection-in/on-action) about their practice that is intuitive and when articulated can be useful to others who are in the same profession. As Schön (1983: 49) noted:

> If the model of Technical rationality is incomplete, in that it fails to account for practical competence in 'divergent' situations, so much the worse for the model. Let us search instead for an epistemology of practice implicit in the artistic, intuitive processes which some practitioners do bring to situations of uncertainty, instability, uniqueness and value conflict.

I have attempted to discover the most cited scholars outside TESOL and in the field of general education who research the concept of reflection and RP to see how they have defined these terms, and in fact, what terms they use in their research as well as who has influenced their definitions of these terms. Table 1.1 outlines how 22 of the most cited scholars in general education research related to the concept of RP have approached definitions of reflection and reflective practice; in particular I specify the term each of them used in their research, how they defined or described the term they used, and which scholar this description was influenced by. I present them in alphabetical order.

In general, the majority of general education articles focus on both the cognitive aspect of reflection (as a mental process) and on the meta-cognitive aspect (examining teachers' own beliefs and practices). Freese (1999: 898), for example, describes reflection as 'the process of making sense of one's experiences by deliberately and actively examining one's thoughts and actions to arrive at new ways of understanding oneself as a teacher.' In addition, Korthagen & Wubbels (1995: 55) state that 'reflection is the mental process of structuring or restructuring an experience, a problem or existing knowledge or insights.' These examples illustrate reflection as a mental process (cognitive) as well as an examination of one's experiences or knowledge (meta-cognitive). Also, some researchers (Parra et al., 2015; Jay & Johnson, 2002) use Dewey's (1910/1933: 9) description of reflection as 'the active, persistent, and careful consideration of any belief or supposed form of knowledge in light of the grounds that support it.' Although less frequent, some articles depict the affective aspect of reflection. For example, Boud et al. (1985: 19) suggest that 'reflection is an important human activity in which people recapture their experience, think about it, mull it over and evaluate it.' In this particular instance, human activity refers to the emotional aspect of humans. Additionally, Jay & Johnson (2002: 75) maintain that 'reflection involves intuition, emotion, and passion and is not something that can be neatly packaged as a set of techniques for teachers to use.' These researchers acknowledge that in order for reflection to occur, the affective aspect is needed. Similarly, two articles incorporate the learner aspect in their definition of 'reflection' (Collin et al., 2013; Lyons, 1998).

As table 1.1 thus illustrates, most of these scholars cite Dewey's work followed much less by Schön, with some citing both scholars as having influenced their definitions and perceptions of the terms that most used: 'reflection' and 'reflective practice'. Indeed, the influence of Dewey's work can be seen throughout these studies since these various definitions seem to share or incorporate certain aspects of his definition of reflection. For instance, Brookfield (1995: 214) describes reflective practice as having 'its roots in the Enlightenment idea that we can stand outside of ourselves and come to a clearer understanding of what we do and who we are by freeing ourselves of distorted ways of reasoning and acting.' Although there is no explicit connection to Dewey's work, the notion of 'standing outside of ourselves and coming to a clearer understanding of what we do and who we are' can be linked to Dewey, especially when he said: 'the self is not something

Table 1.1 Prominent Definitions of Reflection/Reflective Practice in General Education

Study	Term Used	Description	Influence
Boud et.al. (1985)	reflection	'human activity in which people recapture their experience, think about it' p. 19	Dewey
Brookfield (1995)	reflective practice	'we can stand outside ourselves and come to a clearer understanding of what we do' p. 214	Dewey
Calderhead (1989)	reflection	'a moral as well as rational process of deciding what ought to be done in a practical situation' p. 44	Dewey
Collin et al. (2013)	reflective practice	'a process concerning a particular object and in view of achieving a particular goal or rationale' p. 105	Dewey
Copeland et al. (1993)	reflective practice	'a process of solving practice problems and reconstructing meaning' p. 349	Dewey Schön
Cressey et al. (2006)	reflection	'a complex, multi-faceted and messy process ... a discursive way of creating a space for focusing on problematic situations' p. 2	Dewey Brookfield
Freese (1999)	reflection	'the process of making sense of one's experiences by examining one's thoughts and actions to arrive at new ways of understanding oneself as a teacher ... reflection can be enhanced with another individual' p. 898	Dewey Schön
Hatton & Smith (1995)	reflection	'more than constructive self-criticism of one's actions with a view to improvement; it implies acceptance ideology' p. 35	Dewey Schön
Jay & Johnson (2002)	reflection	'process both individual and collaborative, involving experience and uncertainty.... Through reflection, one reaches newfound clarity, on which one bases changes in action or disposition.' p. 76	Dewey Schön
Kemmis (1985)	reflection	'a political act, which either hastens or defers the realization of a more rational, just and fulfilling society' p. 140. 'Reflection is action-oriented, social and political. Its "product" is praxis' p. 141	Dewey
Korthagen (1993)	reflection	'reflection involves not simply a sequence of ideas, but a consequence – a consecutive ordering in such a way that each determines the next at its proper outcome, while each leans back on its predecessors' p. 317	Dewey
Korthagen & Wubbels (1995)	reflection	'the mental process of structuring or restructuring an experience, a problem or existing knowledge or insights' p. 55	Dewey
Larrivee (2000)	reflective thinking	'way of thinking that accepts uncertainty and acknowledges dilemmas while ascribing less significance to the role of self in reflective process' p. 294	Dewey

Loughran (2002)	reflective practice	'ability to frame and reframe the practice setting, to develop and respond to this framing through action so that practitioner's wisdom-in-action is enhanced and professional knowledge is encouraged' p. 42	Schön
Lyons (1998)	reflection	'Connections are made between one's values, purposes, and actions towards engaging students successfully in their own meaningful learning' p. 126. 'ways in which teachers nterrogate their teaching practices the evolution and interrogations of more complex ways of engaging in critical examination of one's teaching practices' pp. 115–116	Schön
Mezirow (1998)	reflection	'turning back on experience: simple awareness of an object, event or state, letting one's thoughts wander over something, taking something into consideration, or imagining alternatives' p. 185	Dewey
Parra et al. (2015)	reflection	'process that enables faculty to construct knowledge through experience in the classroom' p. 18	Dewey Schön
Rodgers (2002)	reflection	'not an end in itself, but a tool or vehicle used in the transformation of raw experience into meaning-filled theory that is grounded in experience' p. 863	Dewey
Shoffner (2008)	reflection	'to explore an issue and seek a conclusion, grounded in the individual's purposeful engagement in reflective thinking' p. 124	Dewey
Smyth (1989)	reflection	'a ubiquitous, cognitive process, not only reworking tacit knowledge into skill, but providing through symbiotic transformations' p. 27. 'it means to unite cognitively, temporally and spatially disparate elements' p. 277	Dewey Schön
Tremmel (1993)	reflective practice	'paying attention not only to what is going on around you, but also within us, is not only a step towards mindfulness and Zen, but is also the better part of reflective practice' p. 447	Dewey
Urzúa & Vásquez (2008)	reflection	'observable in discourse since reflective practice demands not only a conscious awareness of the craft but an ability to articulate knowledge' p. 1936	Schön
Zeichner & Liston (1996/2014)	reflection	'a holistic way of meeting and responding to problems, a way of being as a teacher' p. 9. 'emancipates us from merely impulsive and routine activity, enables us to direct our actions, enables us to know what we are about when we act' p. 11	Dewey

ready-made, but something in continuous formation through choice of action' (Dewey, 1910/1933: 351).

I also note respectfully, that Stephen Brookfield may not agree with my explicit connections of his work to the work of Dewey and I may be criticized for the perception that I may have 'cherry-picked' some of the quotes above to represent what these scholars have understood to represent their notions about reflection and RP. That said it is also interesting to note that less than half the studies outlined above in table 1.1 actually provided their own definition of 'reflection' or 'reflective practice' preferring to cite Dewey or Schön directly. This has implications for research, researchers, and notions about the theoretical underpinnings of one's approach to reflection and, as I will point out later, it is important for teachers, teacher educators, and other stakeholders to be fully aware of what they are 'buying into' when they cite Dewey or Schön or anyone else when referring to RP. Some scholars make it clear that they are within a particular scholar's theoretical framework whey they define reflection and RP. For example, Zeichner & Liston (1996/2014: 24) returned to Dewey's original ideas when they distinguished between routine action and reflective action and suggested that for teachers 'routine action is guided primarily by tradition, external authority and circumstance' whereas reflective action 'entails the active, persistent and careful consideration of any belief or supposed form of knowledge.'

Perhaps this is one major weakness associated with the whole concept of reflection and RP given that we still go back and cite these two (yes, important) scholars without a full understanding of what their approaches mean or entail; one would wonder if each author/scholar who cites Dewey or Schön as the basis for their own definitions of RP are aware of the theoretical traditions that underpin these two scholars and indeed what theory backs their own attempts to operationalize reflection and RP for their teachers in the trenches? (I address different typologies and approaches in the chapter that follows concerning operationalizing RP.)

Reflective Break

- Are you aware of Dewey's definition of reflection and reflective practice?
- If yes, what do you think is the underlying theoretical understanding associated with his definition?
- Are you aware of Schön's definition of reflection and reflective practice?
- If yes, what do you think is the underlying theoretical understanding associated with his definition?

- Which of the definitions above would you consider most represents your own notions of 'reflection' or 'reflective practice'?
- If none of the above definitions represents anything close to your notions of these terms, how would you define each term?

So far I have presented the major works in the field of general education studies associated with defining the terms reflection and reflective practice; now I will briefly outline some works within the field of TESOL associated with these terms. Farrell (2018a) recently extensively reviewed research on the practices that encourage TESOL teachers to reflect on their practice. Of the 138 studies published in academic peer-reviewed journals (he did not include monographs, book chapters, or books on RP) over a seven-year period (2009–2015), Farrell (2018a) noted that only 52 of those studies defined (with citations) what reflective practice is, and 11 studies attempted to define or very loosely defined the concept by just citing scholars' work, while a total of 75 studies (or over 50% of the total) did not give any definition of the concept but just led into 'reflective practice' without saying what it was. Indeed, many studies used different terms such as *reflection, reflective practice, critical reflection, reflective teaching, reflective action, reflection-in-action, reflection-on-action, reflective practitioner, reflective thinking, reflective inquiry, analytical reflection*, and so on interactively in the sense that they had the same meaning or understanding such as *reflection, reflective practice*.

As Farrell (2018a) noted, this lack of clarity of what the overall concept of, and terms related to, 'reflection' and 'reflective practice' look like in TESOL is problematic because without such clarity in what we mean by the concept of reflection, it is difficult to talk about it in language teacher education programs and courses as well as in in-service courses when we attempt to operationalize it and thus make it more than a mantra to follow. So we need a common language and understanding about what these terms mean before we can encourage TESOL teachers to engage in RP. Thus scholars should be cautious about using these terms without a full understanding of what they mean; as Ecclestone (1996: 153) has correctly pointed out, 'Completely different models of knowledge and learning can underpin ideas about reflective practice.' I hope this will become clearer in the following chapters and especially the next chapter when I outline and discuss different typologies of reflection and their underpinning theories.

In addition, a disturbing fact that emerged from the review of research was that of the citations from the 52 studies (out of 138) that actually defined reflective practice in TESOL, Farrell (2018a) discovered that the 'main' scholars outside TESOL who were cited as a source for the research included Dewey (19 citations) and Schön (22 citations). Other sources cited and within TESOL included the work of Farrell (this author – 10 citations). Although there is a clear connection to Dewey's work, most articles in Farrell's (2018a) review provided only a quotation to describe these terms without any elaboration on the meaning of the quotation. While some articles do provide some elaboration, the meaning of the quotation is not sufficiently explained. It is interesting to note, for example, that Chi (2013: 38) used Dewey's (1910/1933) work to describe reflection: 'reflection involves mulling over a subject in one's mind and giving it serious and constant consideration.' Following this quotation, Chi (2013: 38) adds: 'Dewey advised teachers to examine their beliefs through conscious inquiry into their nature, conditions, and consequences in order to explore and modify them.' Apart from this, there is no additional in-depth explanation or elaboration on Dewey's quotation. Again we can see (as in the field of general education) there is still a lack of clarity in definitions of what reflection and reflective practice is in the field of TESOL.

When comparing the ways in which 'reflection' is defined or conceptualized within and outside the field of TESOL, several patterns emerge. Most frequently, definitions of 'reflection' have focused sharply on the cognitive and meta-cognitive aspects. In contrast, the social, affective, and learner aspects have rarely been incorporated in articles relating to TESOL or General Education. However, the moral and critical aspects of reflection have been included in General Education articles, whereas in TESOL, no articles included the moral aspect and very few articles discussed the critical aspect. That has led my own research and quest for understanding of this interesting yet complex topic and how I would define the terms.

Reflective Break

- Why do you think the field of TESOL has not included the moral and critical aspects of reflection in any definitions?
- As a TESOL teacher how would you now define reflective practice?

Levels of Reflection

The above definitions (or explanations of definitions) also all vary in some way in terms of the levels of their depth of reflection (some call this hierarchical levels of reflection) from a description of what it is teachers do, to explanation and focus, as well as the level of critical and moral aspects of the nature of reflection undertaken. As readers will note from reading this chapter on defining reflective practice and the chapter that follows on different typologies of what RP entails, the concept has been approached by different scholars in two main ways: as an *iterative process* or in terms of *different levels* of reflection. As an iterative dimension, reflection is seen in terms of a process of moves triggered by experience of some issue that leads a teacher to take some action, and examples of these such as Boud et al. (1985), Schön (1983), and others are explained in detail in chapter 2. A levels approach to defining reflection involves a vertical dimension that has levels representing different depths of analysis from surface descriptions to more deeper critical analyses that are often harder to reach. Thus I address different typologies in different ways in this book by separating them by those scholars who distinguish between different levels of reflection (vertical) in this chapter, and those who conceptualize reflection as an iterative process in their typologies of reflection in the chapter that follows. Before you continue reading, I encourage you to check your level of reflection as outlined in the reflective break that follows.

Reflective Break

- *Check your level*: although the following questions are not very scientific they will nonetheless get you started on considering what level of reflection you may be at and this will help facilitate a discussion on what level you want to reflect at (adapted from Taggart & Wilson, 1998). Read the statements below and for each statement, circle the number of the indicator that best reflects your agreement and give yourself points for each answer as follows: *4=Almost always; 3=Regularly; 2=Situational; 1=Seldom.*
    1. I can identify a problem or puzzle related to my practice　　4 3 2 1
    2. I analyze a problem/puzzle based upon the needs of the student　　4 3 2 1
    3. I seek evidence which supports or refutes my decision (in # 2)　　4 3 2 1
    4. I view problems/puzzles in an ethical context　　4 3 2 1

5. I use an organized approach to solving problems/puzzles   4 3 2 1
6. I am intuitive in making judgments   4 3 2 1
7. I creatively interpret problems/puzzles   4 3 2 1
8. My actions vary with the context of the problem/puzzle   4 3 2 1
9. I feel most comfortable with a set routine   4 3 2 1
10. I have strong commitment to values related to my practice   4 3 2 1
11. I am responsive to the educational needs of my students   4 3 2 1
12. I review my personal aims and actions related to my practice   4 3 2 1
13. I am flexible in my thinking related to my practice   4 3 2 1
14. I have a questioning nature   4 3 2 1
15. I welcome peer review of my professional actions   4 3 2 1
16. I use innovative ideas in my lessons   4 3 2 1
17. My teaching focus is on my lesson objectives   4 3 2 1
18. There is no best approach to teaching   4 3 2 1
19. I have the skills necessary to be a successful teacher   4 3 2 1
20. I have the content necessary to be a successful teacher   4 3 2 1
21. I consciously modify my teaching to meet my students' needs   4 3 2 1
22. I complete tasks adequately   4 3 2 1
23. I understand concepts, procedures and skills related to practice   4 3 2 1
24. I consider the social implications of my practice   4 3 2 1
25. I set long-term teaching goals   4 3 2 1
26. I self-monitor my teaching   4 3 2 1
27. I evaluate my teaching effectiveness   4 3 2 1
28. My students usually meet my instructional objectives   4 3 2 1
29. I write about my practice regularly   4 3 2 1
30. I engage in action research   4 3 2 1

Scoring Procedure: Add up all the circled numbers: Total_____
What level was most evident? *Descriptive=Below 75; Conceptual=75 to 104; Critical=105 to 120.*

• What attributes do you consider to be most indicative of a reflective practitioner?
• Write examples of each statement above: create possible examples or actions derived from possession of each statement.
• What level should teachers reflect at?

The next section discusses some of the different models (there are many) associated with levels of reflection as outlined in particular approaches in the field of general education, in chronological order: Van Manen (1977); Grimmett et al. (1990); Day (1993); Hatton & Smith (1995); Zeichner & Liston (1996/2014); Valli (1997), so that readers can get an idea of what these levels are and where they came from.

Van Manen

Van Manen (1977), who expanded the work of Habermas' *Theory of Cognitive Interests*, was first to suggest a reflective practice framework that outlined different levels of reflective thought. He noted three different levels of reflection: technical rationality or methodological problems and theory development to achieve objectives; deliberative rationality or pragmatic placement of theory into practice; and critical rationality, or value commitment toward educational process. He observed that teachers are usually only expected to solve problems efficiently with no deep reflections on beliefs of what they were doing. According to Van Manen (1977: 209), the educational system was 'an instrumental preoccupation with techniques, control, and with means-end criteria of efficiency and effectiveness.' Thus teachers had to make choices about solutions made available to them with questioning their meanings to them. Van Manen's pragmatic view led him to encourage teachers to critically evaluate these prescribed practices in relation to their outcomes and the assumptions and beliefs informing them. At the deepest level of reflection he encouraged teachers to engage in 'critical reflection' which he called a process of thought where the practitioner considered the 'worth of knowledge and the nature of the social conditions necessary for raising the question of worthwhileness in the first place' (Van Manen, 1977: 227). This he noted involved reflection on social justice and freedom in terms of teaching actions and that each teaching action reflected a particular ideology that should be understood. Stephen Brookfield (1995: 17–18) was influenced by this notion and suggested the 'assumption that every teaching action reflected particular ideological perspectives.' I will return to Brookfield's (1995) model of reflection in chapter 2. Later, Van Manen (1991) suggested that reflective practitioners are professionals who reflect in action through constant decision-making guided by the theoretical and practical principles of their discipline, and as such refined his three levels to include:

- *Anticipatory reflection*, which allows a teacher to plan and decide on a course of action, and anticipate future consequences of such action.

- *Active or interactive reflection,* which allows teachers to make immediate decisions during class as events unfold.
- *Recollective reflection,* which allows the teacher to make sense of past experiences and gain new, deeper insight into the meaning of those experiences.

Grimmett et al.

Grimmett et al. (1990) presented a framework for reflection that focuses on reflecting through three different levels on teachers' values and beliefs about education: technical, deliberative, and dialectical. At the technical level they suggested that reflection is an instrumental mediation of actions; at the deliberative level reflection involves deliberation from among competing views; and at the dialectical level reflection involves reconstruction of experience. In terms of teaching it I believe it more interesting to focus on the latter two levels, deliberative reflection and dialectical reflection, as they can also be compared to other scholars' depictions below. For Grimmett et al. (1990) deliberative reflection can help teachers when choosing from alternative ideas and practices of teaching, and situations in practice are examined from several philosophical and practical perspectives before a decision is made on what course of action a teacher can take. In addition, knowledge about teaching is dependent on context and is used to inform, but not direct practice. At the dialectical level of reflection (which can be compared to Van Manen's critical rationality below), teachers are involved in a process of transformation of practice where they question moral and ethical issues of practice. This dialectic between thought and action shows care about knowledge that is useful for students and thus can lead to change in practice.

Day

A seminal article related to levels of reflection by Day (1993) outlined three different levels of reflection: the first (P1) is where teachers focus their reflections on behavioral actions, the second (P2) is where teachers also include justifications of these actions based on current theories of teaching, while at the third level (P3) teachers include the first two and look beyond theories and practices to examine their meaning within ethical, moral, and social ramifications. P1 is where teachers reflect at the level of classroom actions, the reasons for these actions are considered at P2, and justification for the practice of teaching itself is at the level of P3. These three levels are called: *descriptive* (P1: focus on teacher skills), *conceptual* (P2: the rationale for practice), and *critical* (P3: examination of socio-political and moral and ethical results of practice). Jay & Johnson (2002: 77–79) have neatly summarized the three levels outlined above although they use slightly different terminology for the second level (they call it *comparative reflection* and this involves teachers thinking about and questioning their values and beliefs). Day (1993) maintains that most teachers will find themselves planning and acting (constructing practice) at the descriptive level P1, and focusing on observation and this reflection (deconstructing practice) at the comparative level P2 and/or critical level P3; in addition any change that may occur as a result of reflection happens mainly at the P1 action level.

Hatton & Smith

Hatton & Smith (1995) identified three essential levels of reflection: descriptive, dialogical, and critical reflection.

- Descriptive reflection involves reflecting on an event, activity or problem through a simple description of the event or problem without providing any reasons for it.
- Dialogical reflection is a more exploratory process and involves inner dialogue where the teacher steps back to investigate why the event or problem happened and attempts to come up with various solutions.
- Critical reflection involves more meta-cognitive analysis where the teacher considers the wider socio-political context and moral judgment when examining the event, issue, or problem.

Zeichner & Liston

Another approach to reflection, as seen by Zeichner & Liston (1996), relies on reflective practitioners to uncover their own personal theories and make them explicit, although this is very difficult to accomplish. For them, a reflective teacher looks at where their personal theories originated and questions these theories especially as they influence practice. Zeichner & Liston (1996: 44–47) identify a 'five level' model of different dimensions of RP:

1. Rapid reaction: Something happens and a teacher acts instinctively. The teacher is immediate in reflection and action.

2. Repair: The teacher pauses for thought about what happened. May try to repair the situation.
3. Review: The teacher takes time out (hours or days) to reassess the situation.
4. Research: The teacher researches the situation in all its forms (systematic).
5. Retheorize/research: The teacher rethinks the situation in light of what he/she has discovered during the previous four levels of reflection and engages in long-term reflection while looking at what others have done.

Valli

Valli's (1997) model of reflection which is influenced by Schon's (1983 – see chapter 2) and Van Manen's (1977) levels above, includes five levels of reflection: technical, practical, and three levels of moral reflection (deliberative, relational, and critical). Technical reflection is similar to Van Manen's (1977) first level of technical descriptive reflection. The second level of practical reflection is based on Schon's (1983) reflection-*in/on*-action as teachers consider problems and the need for ongoing reframing of these problems in practice (see chapter 2 for more on this). The next levels of deliberative, relational (or personalistic), and critical reflection involve deeper levels of consideration: from considering the diverse needs of the students (deliberative), to awareness of impact of emotions on practice (relational), to a focus on social, moral, political, and ethical issues (critical).

The above conceptualizations of RP in terms of different levels of reflection vary in their levels of explanation and also their levels of criticality, with some being more introspective than others. Ultimately, each model discussed above provides valuable insights into the reflective process and RP and how personal it can become. Some scholars argue that if it is too personal we can be clouded by bias as we do not want consider personal assumptions that may not be pleasant and may cause us pain. Thus certain scholars suggest we should reflect in the company of others so we can be challenged to commit to hunting for our assumptions however unpleasant (Brookfield, 1995). In addition we can see how RP can become very prescriptive if we are not careful, as the different models and levels are underpinned by different values and ideologies that they represent. Teachers as reflective practitioners must reflect on their own values, assumptions, beliefs, and practices, and use the insights gained to make informed decisions about their practice.

Reflective Break

- Some levels of reflection as outlined above are more complex than others. Which ones above do you best identify with and why?
- Which levels of reflective practice (if any) have you engaged with to date in your teacher preparation course?
- Have you previously considered the notion of individual objectivity?
- The levels of reflection discussed above all seem to agree to at least three hierarchical levels of reflection as follows:
  o *Level 1*: The level of a teacher's actions in the classroom – a teacher's observable behaviors.
  o *Level 2*: The theoretical level – what are the theories behind the teacher's behaviors (in level 1)?
  o *Level 3*: The ethical, moral level – what is the role of the wider community in a teacher's theories (level 1) and practices (level 2)?
- Try to give an example of how a teacher could operate at each of the three levels.
- What level of reflection do you find yourself working at now?
- Do you think a teacher should operate (reflect) at any particular level? Explain.

Reflective Practice: A Way of Life

Although not represented or discussed in the brief review above, I have developed my own definition of reflective practice for language educators based on the confusion that I saw in existence with disparate definitions that have different philosophical traditions attached to each. As discussed above, some suggest reflecting on teaching only while others suggest that the impact on the broader society and context where we teach should also be considered. While I agreed with all of the approaches, I noticed that in many of them the processes of reflection were highlighted rather than the person who is teaching or the person-as-teacher. So recently I developed a framework for reflecting on practice that encompasses a holistic approach to reflection, focusing not only on the intellectual, cognitive, and meta-cognitive aspects of practice, but also the spiritual, moral, and emotional non-cognitive aspects of reflection that acknowledge the inner life of teachers (Farrell, 2015b). This framework has five different stages/levels of reflection: *Philosophy*; *Principles*; *Theory*; *Practice*; and *Beyond Practice*. Throughout the reflective process, teachers are encouraged not only to describe but also examine and challenge embedded assumptions at each level, so that they can use the framework as a lens through which they can view their professional (and even personal) worlds, and what has shaped their professional lives as they become more aware of their *philosophy, principles, theories, practices,* and how these impact issues inside and *beyond practice.* Chapter 2 on typologies of RP outlines this in more detail.

I would suggest, therefore, that when defining RP in language education, we take a holistic stance and say it is a systematic examination of one's philosophy, principles, theory, practice, and beyond practice so that we can improve ourselves as teachers and, more importantly, provide optimum learning opportunities for our students. In addition, I embrace Oberg & Blades' (1990: 179) ideas when they suggest that 'Reflection is less a process than a way of being, a way of orienting toward professional practice and toward life.' I will address this in more detail in chapter 3 when I discuss the principles of RP – in particular *principle 6.*

Conclusion

In this chapter we have seen that even though reflection and reflective practice are popular terms in many professions including the field of general education and the field of TESOL, there is still no agreement on what these terms mean or how to define them. This is both good and bad. It is good, because each teacher will have to define it for him/herself, but it is bad because anything goes in terms of all the different definitions in existence. I take an optimistic stance in that when forced to define reflection, teachers will have to look at what it really means for them and this entails looking at all the different typologies and approaches (see chapter 2 for more), the various principles of RP (see chapter 3 for more), the different tools available (see chapter 4 for more), how teachers can self-evaluate through RP (see chapter 6 for more), and how RP can be cultivated in a teacher's life and institution (see chapter 6 for more). I conclude the chapter, however, with my own definition of RP that I developed relatively recently:

> a cognitive process accompanied by a set of attitudes in which teachers systematically collect data about their practice, and, while engaging in dialogue with others, use the data to make informed decisions about their practice both inside and outside the classroom (Farrell, 2015b: 123).

I fully admit that my definition is not conclusive as I continue to gain understanding of this fascinating concept. However, this definition is based on a holistic approach to reflection that I explain in more detail in the chapter that follows.

Chapter 2

Typologies of Reflective Practice

Introduction

As discussed in the previous chapter, just as there are many different definitions of reflection and reflective practice (RP) so too are there many different models of RP, either in terms of the different levels of reflection or in terms of iterations of reflections as represented in different typologies. Each of the typologies of RP discussed in this chapter demonstrates and represents different theoretical traditions and underlying assumptions and beliefs about reflection and reflective practice, as do the different levels of reflection discussed in the previous chapter. As such, researchers, teachers, students, and policy-makers may want to take note of the idea of careful citations to back up their particular assumptions and beliefs, and make sure they mirror what they are thinking in terms of their background traditions and approaches to RP.

The chapter begins with John Dewey's original typology (although I fully realize that it could also be considered as levels of reflection as there is some overlap between levels and iterations of reflection) and then move to Donald Schön's development of Dewey's original reflective inquiry model. Since Schön's work led to reigniting interest in reflective practice, many different typologies that were developed later as a result of it are also discussed in this chapter. Of course, because of space limitations, not all the different typologies that have emerged can be featured here, so the chapter outlines and discusses some main typologies such as those by David Kolb, Graham Gibbs, Christopher Johns, Stephen Brookfield, and Terry Borton. Finally this author's own understanding and interpretation of the concept of RP specifically in the field of teaching English to speakers of other languages (TESOL) is presented through his two typologies of reflection: his early typology as well as his relatively new typology or framework for reflecting on practice for TESOL professionals. This is one of the first frameworks in TESOL that operationalizes reflection based on research in the field of TESOL and is for TESOL teachers specifically. Later in this chapter I will compare many of the approaches and how some of them are similar or different to my own new framework (Farrell, 2015b).

Reflective Break

- What do you know about the work of John Dewey?
- What do you know about the work of Donald Schön?
- What do you know about the work of David Kolb?
- What do you know about the work of Graham Gibbs?
- What do you know about the work of Stephen Brookfield?
- What do you know about the work of Christopher Johns?

John Dewey

Early in the 20th century the great American educator John Dewey (1910, revised edition 1933) suggested that one main aim of education is to help individuals acquire the habit of reflection so that they can engage in intelligent rather than routine thought and action. Dewey's work was situated in post-depression US society and he felt the need for a thinking citizenry in a democratic society. For Dewey (1933), this was the larger purpose of his approach to reflective practice and he called this approach reflective inquiry. It is interesting that instead of out-lining what reflective inquiry was, Dewey (1933) first outlined what it was *not*, and I believe this is useful to all those who would propose a model of or an approach to reflection, given today's lack of clarity and definitional problems associated with the concept (see chapter 1); as Dewey noted, it is not just mulling things over, which unfortunately seems to be a wide interpretation of reflective thinking today. Dewey (1933) observed that many students and teachers were locked in routine thinking and actions that were stifling their creativity because their actions were guided by impulse, tradition, and/or authority. So he suggested that teachers engage in more intelligent (as opposed to routine) thought and action. He maintained that they should act in a more deliberate and intentional manner in their practice, rather than just plugging on every day in a type of mindless approach to teaching.

Thus Dewey (1933: 9) called for teachers to take more reflective action that entails, in his often quoted words: 'active, persistent, and careful consideration of any belief or supposed form of knowledge in light of the grounds that support it

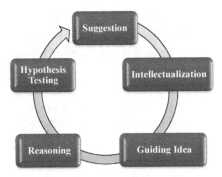

Figure 2.1 Dewey's Reflective Inquiry

and the further consequences to which it leads.' This definition as outlined in the previous chapter has now become somewhat iconic in the literature on RP both in general education and in the field of TESOL. In order that we may be able to give active and careful consideration to any knowledge and especially to examine our teaching beliefs and practices, Dewey (1933) maintained that we should engage in reflective inquiry so that we can be freed from routine thinking and routine actions. Dewey's (1933) reflective inquiry is in fact an evidence-based approach to RP and encourages teachers to avoid making instructional decisions based on impulse or routine; rather, they are encouraged to use the data they have obtained so that they can make more informed decisions about their practice (Farrell, 2015b). Figure 2.1 represents my attempt to illustrate Dewey's reflective inquiry model.

As figure 2.1 illustrates, reflective inquiry has five main phases (although some publications include more and some less) and these are outlined below from the perspective of a TESOL teacher teaching a grammar class (I have also changed the title of each stage slightly from the original to make it applicable for teachers):

- *Suggestion*: A doubtful situation is understood to be problematic, and some vague suggestions are considered as possible solutions. For example, in language teaching (or any field really) we may have noted that our students make many mistakes in grammar while writing. However at this stage we try to avoid making any judgments and we look for alternatives rather than just blaming our students. Perhaps it has something to do with our teaching or the curriculum; we do not know yet.
- *Intellectualization*: The difficulty or perplexity of the problem that has been felt (directly experienced) is intellectualized into a problem to be solved. Here we move from a problem felt to a problem to be solved, so we

begin to refine the problem by asking a question. For example, I now ask if the problem has something to do with my grammar corrections.

- *Guiding Idea*: One suggestion after another is used as a leading idea, or hypothesis; the initial suggestion can be used as a working hypothesis to initiate and guide observation and other operations in the collection of factual material. We now begin to look at some details, for example what I do as a teacher when correcting. So I examine students' papers with my grammar corrections and review the literature on grammar correction which says teachers should not correct all grammar mistakes. As a result I decide the problem must be something to do with my corrections so I have to change them.

- *Reasoning*: Reasoning links present and past ideas and helps elaborate the supposition that reflective inquiry has reached, or the mental elaboration of the idea or supposition. So through reasoning I decide to implement selective grammar corrections but am not sure yet if this will work.

- *Hypothesis Testing*: The refined idea is reached, and the testing of this refined hypothesis takes place; the testing can be by overt action or in thought (imaginative action). I begin now to test and monitor my selective grammar corrections by action and observation in practice. If successful, then I can draw strong positive conclusions to my solutions. If this fails, they I must try some other solution and see what may happen (from Farrell, 2015b).

The reflective inquiry stages are presented as circular and somewhat itera-tive, although Dewey did not do so at the time, because each step influences the other and, as Dewey noted, they should not be taken as linear in that teachers can only think about one stage before moving to the next and so on. Rather, Dewey acknowledged that reflective inquiry can be a bit messy and that teachers can jump back and forth between stages as they attempt to solve a problem. In fact, he rec-ommended that teachers continuously move within the model until the 'problem' they are inquiring about is solved; in fact according to him the problem must be solved, and as such there is no uncertainty. As Dewey (1933: 275) relayed:

> The teacher must have his mind free to observe the mental responses and movement of the student.... The problem of the students is found in the subject matter; the problem of the teacher is what the minds of the students are doing with the subject matter.

Dewey maintained that such 'reflective thinking' (or, as he described it, suspending immediate judgment) within his reflective inquiry model is not easy and even sometimes leads to unpleasant feelings and can be dangerous, because teachers must actively challenge their taken-for-granted ways of doing things and thus be taken out of their comfort zones as they are forced to look at themselves. It is not easy to enter such a world of self-criticism by examining closely what we actually do in our classes rather than what we think we do, and then articulating what we can do better as a result of the evidence we have unearthed. In fact, as we all know, it is much easier for us to follow routine each day rather than dig into our practice and create an uncertain state of mind as a result; it is easier to avoid all the hassle.

Dewey's (1933) reflective inquiry model is actually the precursor to action research cycles that have become very popular in recent TESOL literature that encourages language teachers to examine their practice. My own work in RP has been and still is influenced by Dewey's (1933) reflective inquiry cycle because it encourages an evidence-based approach to RP rather than the commonsense approach to reflection of just thinking about what we do without gathering any evidence or taking any action. Later Boud et al. (1985) reworked Dewey's five phases of reflection into three (although they have sub-phases that could be counted) and put more emphasis on emotions or the affective activities practitioners use to explore their experiences in order to arrive at new understandings of their practice. Boud et al. (1985) called this 'attending to feelings' during the experience as their second stage or level of reflection, the first being anticipation of the experience and the last a consolidation after the experience.

Reflective Break

- What is your understanding of Dewey's reflective inquiry?
- What is your approach to routine in your practice?
- Do you think that teachers should follow routine?
- Go through each of Dewey's stages of reflective inquiry as you reflect on a recent teaching experience, and write your responses in a journal.
- Do you agree with Boud et al.'s (1985) inclusion of emotions in the reflective cycle? If yes, where should teachers include this affective component?

Donald Schön

There was a lull for many years after Dewey's 'discovery' of reflection in education (and what some would call revolutionary thoughts on the need for both students and teachers to reflect on their practices) until the 1980s which saw the emergence of the work of Donald Schön (1983, 1987). Some scholars maintain that imprints of John Dewey's work above are ever present in the work of Donald Schön; in fact, Schön's PhD dissertation (Yale, Philosophy, 1955) was focused on an analysis of Dewey's 'Theory of Inquiry'. Although he did not refer to Dewey in his work, this would lead Schön to take a more pragmatic (rather than theoretical) approach to RP in most of his later work.

It is interesting to note that initially Schön did not work much with teachers, but rather within organizations in general as he was interested in how practitioners in these organizations viewed their work. Although Schön looked at many aspects of organizational behavior, it is probably safe to say that for educators his focus on the notion of practitioner-generated intuitive practice was of most interest. Schön (1983: vii) made this clear in his early influential book, *The reflective practitioner: How professionals think in action*, when he stated:

> We are in need of inquiry into the epistemology of practice. What is the kind of knowing in which competent practitioners engage? How is professional knowing like and unlike the kinds of knowing in academic textbooks, scientific papers and journals?

In the 1970s Schön had teamed up with Chris Argyris while at MIT and developed the (now famous) notion of single loop and double loop learning (Argyris & Schön, 1974). Single loop learning is defined as planning, teaching, and testing, but as they noted this remains at the tacit level of learning because our theories in use are deeply entrenched in the individual and thus subconscious. Thus if action fails to solve a problem, the individual never questions his or her underlying assumptions about a problem and learning remains reflexive or single-looped. In double loop learning, the individual will not only examine the action itself but also question the underlying assumptions that impacted the action in the first place. Thus double loop learning occurs where thinking, practice, and problems between the two are raised to an explicit level where they can be accessed. This collaboration with Chris Argyris led Schön to focus on professional learning within organizations and how to develop critical self-reflection that was to influence the work he is most recognized for and his idea of practitioners reflecting-*in*-action. (I would suggest that Dewey was concerned mostly with practitioners reflecting-*on*-action, or reflection after the event.)

More specifically, Schön (1983, 1987) was very interested in how professionals 'know' what they 'know' through their practice because he was convinced that they 'know' more than they can articulate. In other words he was interested in getting practitioners to articulate what they 'know' and 'do' by getting them to engage in what he called reflection-*in*-action, or as I would suggest 'thinking-on-their-feet'. Engaging in reflection-*in*-action involves examining beliefs and experiences and how they connect to theories-in-use. However, in order to engage in reflection-*in*-action Schön (1983, 1987) maintained that practitioners must become aware of their knowing-*in*-action and this process moves beyond the usual established ideas as practitioners build up and draw on a collection of images, ideas, and actions.

Applying Schön's (1983, 1987) work to teaching (although he did not write directly about teachers), knowing-*in*-action would be crucial because teachers cannot possibly question every action or reaction while they are teaching otherwise they would not be able to get through a class. So a teacher's knowing-*in*-action works similarly to when we recognize a face in a crowd but we do not list or try to consciously piece together each separate facial feature that makes a person recognizable to us. We do not consciously think, 'Could that be...?' – we just know. In addition, if you were asked to describe the features that prompted this recognition, it might be difficult because, as Schön (1983) has pointed out, that type of information usually remains at the subconscious level of our thoughts. However, when a new situation or event occurs and our established routines do not work for us, then according to Schön (1983), teachers use reflection-in-action to cope. Reflection-in-action involves a reflective conversation where the practitioner is listening to the 'situation's backtalk'. Although he did not actually produce what would be called a 'model' of RP, I attempt to produce one in Figure 2.2, as an illustration of

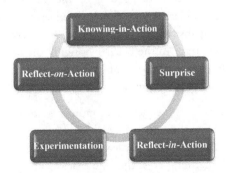

Figure 2.2 Schön's Approach to Reflective Practice

Schön's (1987) approach to RP (I realize that this figure is my own interpretation of his work).

Figure 2.2 illustrates a five-stage reflection process representation of Schön's (1983, 1987) approach to RP that includes his now famous reflection-*in*-action, but I also maintain that his sequence of reflection actually ends in reflection-*on*-action (similar to Dewey). This model shows the practitioner moving along a 'causal chain' in a sequence of moments in a *process* of reflection-*in*-action in which the practitioner attempts to solve a problem (the *cause* of reflection-*in*-action) as follows (I present this for TESOL teachers again teaching a grammar class, as above with Dewey's model):

- A situation develops which triggers spontaneous, routine responses (such as in knowing-in-action): for example, a student cannot answer an easy grammar question that he was able to during the previous class, such as identifying a grammar structure.
- Routine actions by the teacher (i.e., what the teacher has always done) do not produce a routine response and instead produce a surprise for the teacher: the teacher starts to explain how the student had already identified this grammar structure in the previous class and wonders what has happened now. The teacher asks the student if anything is the matter and the student says he forgets the answer.
- This surprise response gets the teacher's attention and leads to reflection within an action: the teacher reacts quickly to try to find out why the student suddenly 'forgets' a grammar structure the teacher knows he has no trouble understanding. The teacher asks the student directly to explain what is happening and the student begins to cry.
- Reflection now gives rise to on-the-spot experimentation by the teacher: the student may or may not explain why he or she is crying. The teacher will take some measures (depending on the reaction or non-reaction) to help solve the problem: ignore the situation, empathize with the student, help the student answer the question by modeling answers, and so forth.
- This eventually leads to the teacher bringing the event outside the class for later reflection or reflection-on-action, similar to Dewey, as the practitioner thinks about the events after the event.

According to Schön these sequences of moments are all present and lead to reflection-*in*-action while the teacher is teaching. I have taken his model one step further and suggest that this eventually leads back to reflection-*on*-action after the lesson, when the teacher reflects *on* the whole process that took place including what happened during the lesson. In this case Schön says that practitioners engage in a process of *problem setting* rather than problem solving. For Schön, each 'situation of practice' is unique and distinct and therefore not open to the usual routine approach used to solve the problem, and this all depends on individual awareness of the 'situation'. As Clarke (1995: 245) explains: 'This conversation between the practitioner and the setting provides the data which may then lead to new meanings, further reframing, and plans for further action.'

Schön (1983) noted that Dewey encouraged teachers to reflect on their practice after the fact, or reflection-*on*-action. However, Schön, like Dewey, maintained that reflection begins in professional practice some of which may be 'messy' and confusing, and so even though teachers may have obtained their subject matter knowledge (their theoretical knowledge), this does not explain what actual classroom practice is because teachers obtain their tacit knowledge from these real-classroom experiences. As such, teachers must engage in reflection-*in*-action (thinking on their feet) as well as reflection-*on*-action (after the class) and these should be documented in some manner so that they can also help teachers to reflect-*for*-action (see Farrell, 2004, 2015b).

Although I have presented an illustration of what I would think a 'Schönian model' of RP is that includes more than his famous reflection-*in*-action, other scholars have suggested that his work did not actually produce a concise model beyond encouraging practitioners to reflect while they practice. In other words, they maintain that Schön did not offer enough structure (that other typologies do) for practitioners in this approach to RP. I disagree because his work has been groundbreaking in so many different ways and for me his most important contribution to RP was his practical application of reflection for everyday professionals to implement and develop as they perform their particular roles in society. Simply, Schön would say that 'professionals matter' – or for education, 'teachers matter' – and that we should develop an approach that can help professionals/teachers to better perform their work as a result of reflection.

Reflective Break

- What is your understanding of the differences between reflection-*in*-action, reflection-*on*-action, and reflection-*for*-action?
- Think of an example where you have separately reflected-in-action and also one when you reflected-on-action, and compare the two. Did reflection-*in*-action lead to reflection-*on*-action and/or reflection-*for*-action?
- Go through each phase of Schön's cycle as you reflect on a recent teaching experience and write your responses in a journal.

David Kolb

Although not called reflection or reflective practice, David Kolb's (1984) influential theory of experiential learning attempts to produce an overall typology of learning and the idea of a central role of a practitioner's experience in that learning process. Kolb's (1984) model is a four-stage experience cycle that follows the sequence: concrete experience, reflective observation, abstract conceptualization, and active experimentation (figure 2.3). Concrete experience is where a practitioner describes an experience. Observation is where the practitioner explains if the experience was positive or negative. Formation of abstract concepts is where the practitioner describes what worked well or did not work well. Testing concepts in new situations is where the practitioner asks if he or she would change or do anything differently in light of the new information.

As stated above, Kolb attempted to incorporate the concept of experience and its role in the process of learning, and his 'Four-Stage Experiential Learning Cycle' (figure 2.3) actually originated from the Lewinian Experiential Learning Model rather than any reflective practice model. As Kolb (1984: 38) noted, 'Learning is the process whereby knowledge is created through the transformation of experience.' This is interesting theoretical background to Kolb's (1984) work and it is important again to remember that each approach has some underpinning theory (in this case that of Kurt Lewin), especially as Kolb is often cited in the literature on RP. In addition it should also be noted that Kolb initially collaborated with Ron Fry (Kolb & Fry, 1975) as they mapped out these four phases of reflection: (1) experience, (2) observation, (3) conceptualization, and (4) experimentation.

However, some scholars who have (re)interpreted this model within the concept of reflective practice have suggested that it can be summarized into a

Figure 2.3 Kolb's (1984) 'Four-Stage Experiential Learning Cycle'

four-stage reflective plan such as: *do it, reflect on it, read up on it*, and *plan the next stage*. For example, applying this model within an educational setting, we note that a teacher first teaches a lesson (*do it*) and then reflects on what went well or not so well from the teacher's perspective (*reflect on it*). Then the teacher attempts to get more information about the issue by reading or doing searches and speaking to other teachers about it (*read up on it*). After this, the teacher plans how to implement this new knowledge in the next lesson (*plan the next stage*).

This reinterpretation of Kolb's (1984) experiential model into a reflective model of *do, reflect, read*, and *plan* shows how Kolb's work combines reflection with experience and helps teachers, and especially novice teachers, to structure their reflections early in their careers by following this step-by-step process. In fact, the cycle can begin anywhere: for example, if the teacher wants to read about some issue first and then follow the cycle. In such a manner teachers can begin to take more responsibility for their own development early in their careers.

Many authors/scholars within the field of education have since built on and developed this reflective model to promote reflective practice. For example, when developing his ALACT model of RP, Korthagen (1985) adapted Kolb & Fry's (1975) model, and this newer version has been used in many teacher education programs since. ALACT is an acronym standing for: Action; Looking; Awareness; Creating; Trial. This cycle consists of five phases: (1) Action, (2) Looking back on the action, (3) Awareness of essential aspects, (4) Creating alternative methods of action, and (5) Trial – which itself is a new action and thus the starting point of a new cycle. Another cycle that extended Kolb's was developed by Graham Gibbs (1988), outlined in the next section.

Reflective Break

- What is your understanding of Kolb's (1984) 'Four-Stage Experiential Learning Cycle'?
- How is this related to reflective practice?
- How can you apply this model to your reflections and teaching?
- Is reflective practice about teachers reflecting on what works or does not work well in their classes or are there also other aspects to it? Explain.
- Go through each phase of Kolb's cycle as you reflect on a recent teaching experience and write your responses in a journal.

Graham Gibbs

Graham Gibbs (1988) also developed a typology of RP, or a cycle as he called it, within the field of nursing. This model is greatly influenced by Kolb's (1984) experiential learning cycle but whereas Kolb has four stages in his cycle, Gibbs has six. The extra stages added in Gibbs' model, developed to help with the professional development of nursing practitioners, signal his desire to include an affective component to reflection. Gibbs' (1988) reflective cycle thus includes the idea of emotional reflection or how emotions impact a practitioner's reflections on an experience (figure 2.4).

Figure 2.4 Gibbs' (1988) Reflective Cycle

As can been seen in figure 2.4, the first stage of Gibbs' reflective cycle is a description of the experience, followed by the next stage where the feelings of the practitioner are considered, then the third stage where the practitioner evaluates how good or bad the experience has been. This is followed by an analysis of the experience to suggest what was learned; then the practitioner draws a conclusion about what could have been done differently, based on the reflections so far; and finally an action plan is drawn up for what is to be done the next time. Gibbs introduces a stage involving the identification of emotions during an experience or event, and also extends Kolb's fourth stage to include a conclusion and action plan.

Reflective Break

- What is your understanding of Gibbs' reflective cycle?
- Do you think it is important to include an emotional component to reflecting on practice? Why or why not?
- Which of the two typologies (Kolb or Gibbs) would you use and why?
- Go through each stage of Gibbs' cycle as you reflect on a recent teaching experience and write your responses in a journal.

Christopher Johns

Chris Johns, also interested in developing the concept of reflective practice in the nursing profession, further developed combinations of Gibbs' work. He suggested that reflective practice is a way of being (see also principle 6 in chapter 3) and encouraged nursing practitioners to actively engage in reflection during their daily practice. Essentially he suggested a typology of reflective practice that moves from 'doing' reflection towards reflection as a 'way of being' within everyday practices. Johns' work was influenced by Carper's (1978) ideas of exploring aesthetics and personal knowing and how exploration of these can change or improve practice. Johns' (1995) model of reflection created five different cues to guide nursing practitioners in their reflections: *aesthetics, personal, ethics, empirics,* and *reflexivity.* The first cue, *aesthetics,* gets practitioners to reflect on what they were trying to do, why, what the consequences were, and how other people felt at that time. This is followed by the second cue, *personal,* and asks how practitioners felt in that situation

Figure 2.5 Johns' (1995) Model of Structured Reflection

and what influenced their decisions. This is followed by a cue on *ethics* where practitioners reflect on how their actions matched (or not) their beliefs. The fourth cue is *empirics* where practitioners are asked what knowledge informed their decisions. Finally, *reflexivity* leads practitioners to consider how the event connects with other experiences. Before the practitioners are asked these five questions they must fully describe the experience or event in detail. Johns' (1995) model of structured reflection has also often been illustrated in the following stages: description of experience, reflection, influencing factors, could I have dealt with it differently, and learning (figure 2.5).

It is interesting to note that Johns has maintained that reflection within the nursing profession is about personal growth rather than better patient outcomes. After meeting him at a conference, I can see he is the living embodiment of his approach to reflective practice.

Reflective Break

- What is your understanding of Johns' (1995) Model of Structured Reflection?
- Do you think reflection is a way of being?
- Go through each stage of Johns' cycle as you reflect on a recent teaching experience and write your responses in a journal.

Stephen Brookfield

Stephen Brookfield is usually associated with the important aspect of critical reflection for teachers and this is one of the least applied areas of reflection to language teaching. Brookfield (1995) gave some reasons why critical reflection is important: we can take informed actions; it helps teachers develop a rationale for practice; it helps teachers avoid self-laceration; it grounds teachers emotionally; it enlivens classrooms. Most of these reasons include teachers being able to justify what they do and why they do it and thus not always blame themselves, as they have done the best they can. In others words, after systematically exploring their practice they are more grounded emotionally because they do not leave things to chance.

More specifically, Brookfield (1995) suggested that critically reflective teachers should examine the assumptions that underlie their practices and, in order to do this, must look at what they do, or their practice. He suggested that teachers can examine their practice through four 'critical lenses' as follows: teacher lens; learner

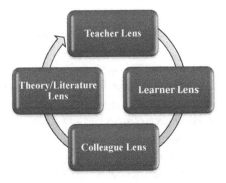

Figure 2.6 Brookfield's Critical Lenses

lens; colleague lens; theories and literature lens. Although I am not aware of a particular illustration that Brookfield has even used to display this typology, I have nevertheless taken the liberty of attempting to represent this model in figure 2.6.

My interpretation of the Brookfield's critical lenses is as follows:

- *Teacher lens*: teachers examine what they do in their classrooms: not what they think they do, but what they actually do. I have discovered over the years what teachers think they do and what they actually do is not always the same, so they have to collect evidence about what they do by recording their classes, transcribing and reflecting on the results. This self-reflection can also involve others and so ties into all the other lenses that Brookfield mentions.

- *Learner lens*: teachers can ask their students what they think they do in class. Brookfield suggests they use the critical incident questionnaire (CIQ) to help see their practice through their students' eyes. This consists of five questions, each of which asks students to write down some details about events that happened in the class that week. The questions are:

  1. At what moment in the class this week did you feel most engaged with what was happening?
  2. At what moment in the class this week did you feel most distanced from what was happening?
  3. What action that anyone (teacher or student) took in class this week did you find most affirming and helpful?
  4. What action that anyone (teacher or student) took in class this week did you find most puzzling or confusing?

5. What about the class this week surprised you the most? (This could be something about your own reactions to what went on, or something that someone did, or anything else that occurs to you.)

In addition to Brookfield's questions above that are used in general education settings, I have used a refined form of these over the years to ask ESL/EFL students at the end of classes the following three questions:

o   What did we do in class today?
o   What was easy for you?
o   What was difficult for you?

By asking our language learners about their understanding of our teaching we are inviting them to engage in reflective learning and that can help them achieve their learning aims. It also helps teachers to discover any blind spots that can go unseen in our teaching and our learning and development as teachers.

- *Colleague lens*: teachers can also talk to and with colleagues and ask them what they do in similar situations, and perhaps ask them to act as critical friends and observe classes. Our colleagues can act as mirrors, as John Fanselow (1988) has pointed out, by telling us what they saw and indeed by relating their own experiences with similar events. In this manner we can broaden our own understanding of our teaching and decide what is best for us.

- *Theory/literature lens*: teachers can also read about what others have done. As Brookfield notes, theory can help us 'name' our practice, especially if we think we are the only ones approaching our practice in such a manner. Brookfield (1995: 36) points out that 'Studying theory can help us realize that what we thought were signs of our personal failings as teachers can actually be interpreted as the inevitable consequence of certain economic, social, and political processes.'

Reflective Break

- What is your understanding of Brookfield's Critical Lenses?
- Go through each of Brookfield's four lenses as you reflect on a recent teaching experience and write your responses in a journal. As you do so, think about the ways you can obtain the views of your students; then find a colleague who will act as a critical friend to explore the experience with you.

Terry Borton

Terry Borton's (1970) Developmental Framework (further developed by Rolfe et. al., 2001) is probably the simplest of all typologies in terms of providing structure especially for novice teachers. This model asks practitioners to answer three simple questions: *What? So what? Now what?* The 'what' question is the basic descriptive question followed by the 'so what' which seeks reflection on the practitioner's theory and the 'now what' final question which seeks some kind of reflective action. Figure 2.7 represents Borton's framework.

This model places reflection at three different levels: description, theory, and action. For description or the 'what' question, teachers can ask questions such as: What was the issue/problem? What was my role? What happened (results)? What did I do? For the 'so what' question, teachers can theorize by asking such questions as: What was I thinking during the incident? What did I learn? What was important about this incident? Then in the action-oriented phase or the 'now what' phase, teachers can synthesize by asking questions such as: What do I need to do now? What do I need to do to resolve this problem? What might be the results of my actions?

I include this early model with all the other typologies because it has been noted as offering practitioners, especially novice practitioners, a simple, structured way to reflect on their practice. However, as you will read later, although I see value in providing such a structure, it can also lead to a place where reflective typologies offer very narrow approaches and may reduce reflection to more ritualistic and mechanical modes that can result in the development of checklists that defeat the original spirit of reflection against using such checklists to describe practice. Indeed, this is the very reason why I developed my own more recent typology of reflective practice: as an answer to these one-dimensional approaches that confine reflection to a retrospective role such as simply answering Borton's (1970) three questions. I discuss this in more detail in the sections that follow.

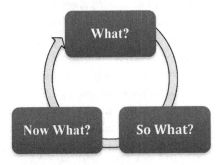

Figure 2.7 Borton's (1970) Developmental Framework

Reflective Break

- What is your understanding of Borton's (1970) Developmental Framework?
- Go through each of Borton's questions as you reflect on a recent teaching experience and write your responses in a journal.

Thomas Farrell

Dewey's and Schön's legacies are important because they moved the concept of reflection far beyond everyday simple wonderings about a situation (or mulling over something without taking action) to a more rigorous form of reflective thinking whereby a teacher systematically investigates a perceived problem in order to discover a workable solution over time. I realize that I am attracted to their work because they were very pragmatic in their approaches so that they could help practicing teachers on the frontlines. Indeed, I made some early attempts to develop some kind of model or framework for reflecting on practice that would encompass both Dewey and Schön's work where teachers are encouraged to engage in evidence-based reflective practice (Farrell, 2004).

Farrell's Early Model

I developed an early model of RP mostly based on my PhD dissertation work that emphasized a practical approach – hence my interest in Schön's (1983) pragmatic approach to reflective practice – with the idea that practicing TESOL teachers would be better able to 'locate themselves within their profession and start to take more responsibility for shaping their practice' (Farrell, 2004: 6) rather than relying on publisher-produced materials and books that were rampant in the TESOL profession at that time. I saw a need for teachers to be able to break away from relying on these badly produced textbooks with teacher guides to *tell* them what they should be doing, and instead take responsibility for their own direction while *teaching their students*. My initial framework attempted to encourage teachers to look at their own practice with other teachers and decide their own future direction in terms of providing opportunities for their students to learn. This framework (Farrell, 2004) of reflective teaching has five components: (1) a range of opportunities and activities, (2) ground rules, (3) provision for four different times or categories of reflection, (4) external input, and (5) trust. Figure 2.8 outlines this model.

Figure 2.8 Farrell's Reflective Practice Framework (2004)

This framework (Farrell, 2004), is explained as follows:

1. *Opportunities.* A range of activities should be provided for teachers to reflect on their work. In this model the activities that were emphasized were group discussions, journal writing, and classroom observations. These activities can be carried out alone, in pairs, or as a group. A group of teachers may decide to do one of the activities or a combination of any or all of them.

2. *Ground rules.* In order to avoid groups or individual teachers just drifting off into something other than reflection, this component suggests a need for a negotiated set of built-in rules or guidelines that each group or pair should follow in order to keep the drifting to a minimum. The model can be adjusted to individual group needs. Indeed, components three through five are actually ground rules that can be built in to the activities. For example, Who will chair the meetings?, and other such related questions. For observations, certain understandings need to be negotiated ahead of time. For example, What are the responsibilities of the observer? Is intervention possible or desirable in the class? Will the class be videotaped, audiotaped, or neither? If you use a video, how will this be analyzed and why? What is to be observed and how? For journal writing, groups/pairs should negotiate the number and frequency of entries and the type of entries. The following list of general questions may help get a writer started: Describe what you do with no judgment. Why do you do it? Should you continue to do it or change it? What do others do? To suggest a set of built-in rules for critical friends while observing is not easy because there must be an element of trust and openness present in order to avoid putting emphasis on the

critical while overlooking the friend. The friend can provide another set of eyes that both support and challenge us to get at deeper reflections of our teaching. To encourage this openness, the initial conversations between critical friends (or all conversations) should be taped and analyzed. This analysis can include the use of questions about their relationship, in terms of type, power structures established, focus of observation, and usefulness. In this way critical friends can negotiate what they want to achieve. Of course, all of the above activities and built-in guidelines cannot be accomplished quickly; like all valuable things, they take time. This introduces the next component of the model.

3. *Time.* For practicing teachers to be able to reflect on their work, time is a very important consideration. Groups can consider four different views/types of time: *Individual, Activity, Development, Period of Reflection:*

   - *Individual*: A certain level of commitment by individual participants in terms of time availability should be negotiated by the group at the start of the process.
   - *Activity*: Associated with the time each participant has to give the project is the time that should be spent on each activity.
   - *Development*: Another aspect of time that is important for teacher self-development groups is the time it takes to develop. Analytical reflection takes time and only progresses at the rate at which individual teachers are ready to reflect critically.
   - *Period of reflection.* The time frame for the project as a whole is important to consider. How long should a group, a pair, or an individual reflect? Having a fixed period in which to reflect allows the participants to know what period during the semester they can devote wholly to reflection.

4. *External input.* The previous three suggestions utilize the idea of probing and articulating personal theories, which is at the center of teacher professional self-development. This involves a process of constructing and reconstructing real teaching experiences, and reflecting on personal beliefs about teaching. However, at this level, reflection only emphasizes personal experiences but what do these mean in the greater professional community? Thus, external input of some kind is necessary to see what other teachers and groups have done. This external input can come from professional journals, other teachers' observations, and book publications of case studies.

5. *Trust.* The above four components of the model can all pose some degree of threat for practicing teachers. Inevitably, there will be a certain level of

anxiety present. Therefore, trust will be a big issue when teachers reflect together and it is necessary that a non-threatening environment be fostered in the group by the individuals themselves.

The most important aspect of this early model (Farrell, 2004) is to encourage reflection and to give teachers the opportunity to reflect. I believe the framework is still relevant today: I have recently used it successfully with experienced TESOL teachers in a teacher reflection group in Canada (e.g., see Farrell, 2014), and it remains worthwhile for teachers wishing to reflect on their practice and especially with a group of teachers. However, I now believe that this framework may be somewhat challenging for novice teachers to enact unless they have mentors to help them. Also I realized that the framework needed to include more about the human aspect of the teacher engaged in RP in a more holistic manner. In other words, I believe that the framework focused too much on practice and too little on the person-as-teacher.

I therefore began to develop a framework that provided more depth to reflection and that included all levels of teachers regardless of their teaching experience. I agree that many of the typologies that I have outlined and discussed in this chapter have admirably provided different types of structured reflection for practitioners by offering probing questions that stimulate reflection. However one main criticism I have of many of these is that they have mostly guided teachers on how to tackle technical issues within the classroom only and have taken a 'fix-it' approach to solving perceived problems without looking at the person who is doing the reflecting, the teacher. This approach puts teaching in a 'bubble' on its own divorced from the person who is teaching and forces a mechanical approach to RP to 'improve' teaching but divorced from the teacher. Indeed, many school administrators have jumped on this bandwagon as they have seized on the idea that reflection can be used as a tool to 'fix' problems (that *they* identify on pre-determined checklists) in teaching. This view sees teachers reverting to being technicians (which defeats the original purpose of RP against such a view of teacher as technician) whose competence is evaluated by the end product of these tools/checklists in terms of the 'changes' they have made in their practice in order to satisfy the administrators' or supervisors' views of what should be done in the classroom. In other words, many models do not look at RP in any holistic manner that includes the person who is reflecting (or person-as-teacher) as well as what the person is reflecting on. I was looking for a way to move the concept of RP to a more holistic approach by providing an overall reflection framework for teachers.

Reflective Break

- What is your understanding of Farrell's (2004) early model of reflection?
- Go through each of Farrell's (2004) five stages as you reflect on a recent teaching experience and write your responses in a journal.
- Do you think that reflective practice should go beyond teachers reflecting on what works or does not work in their classes? If no, why not? If yes, what else should they reflect on?
- Is reflective practice a tool to 'fix' problems in teaching?
- What is the role of the teacher-as-person (if any) in reflective practice?

Farrell's New Framework

I reflected on both Dewey and Schön's work as well as that of other scholars, and revisited my own early framework above following my work with three experienced Canadian ESL teachers (Farrell, 2014), to see if I could develop a more holistic framework of reflective practice for TESOL professionals. I re-examined all the other models and frameworks above to see if these held any useful points earlier missed by me. I also discovered Shapiro & Reiff's (1993) model of reflection from the field of psychology, and this became very influential in the design of my new framework. Shapiro & Reiff (1993) called their model *reflective inquiry on practice* (RIP) and divided the process of reflection into five levels: philosophy, basic theory, theory of technique, technique, and moves. I liked their idea of different levels of reflection and so decided to incorporate something similar into my new framework for language teachers called the Framework for Reflecting on Practice (Farrell, 2015b).

Figure 2.9 Farrell's Framework for Reflecting on Practice (2015b)

As outlined in figure 2.9, the framework has five different stages/levels of reflection: *Philosophy*, *Principles*, *Theory*, *Practice*, and *Beyond Practice*.

Philosophy: This first stage of reflection within the framework examines the 'teacher-as-person' and suggests that professional practice, both inside and outside the classroom, is invariably guided by a teacher's basic philosophy and that this philosophy has been developed since birth. Thus, in order to be able to reflect on our basic philosophy, we need to obtain self-knowledge and we can access this by exploring, examining, and reflecting on our background – from where we have evolved – such as our heritage, ethnicity, religion, socio-economic background, and family and personal values that have combined to influence who we are as language teachers. As such, teachers may talk or write about their own lives and how they think their past experiences may have shaped the construction and development of their basic philosophy of practice. Reflecting on their philosophy of practice can not only help teachers flesh out what has shaped them as human beings and teachers but can also help them move on to the next level, of reflecting on their principles.

Principles: The second stage of the framework includes reflections on teachers' assumptions, beliefs, and conceptions about teaching and learning. All three are really part of a single system, and difficult to separate because they overlap a lot. Although I treat them separately in the framework, I see them as three points along the same continuum of meaning related to our principles. Teachers' practices and their instructional decisions are often formulated and implemented (for the most part subconsciously) on the basis of their underlying assumptions, beliefs, and conceptions because these are the driving force (along with philosophy reflected on at stage one) behind many of their classroom actions.

Theory: Influenced by their reflections on their philosophy and on their principles, teachers can now actively begin to construct their theory of practice. Theory explores and examines the different choices a teacher makes about particular skills taught (or which they think should be taught). In this stage teachers consider the type of lessons they want to deliver on a yearly, monthly, or daily basis. All language teachers have theories, both 'official' theories learnt in teacher education courses and 'unofficial' theories gained through teaching experience. However, not all teachers may be fully aware of these theories, especially their 'unofficial' theories that are sometimes called 'theories-in-use'. Reflections at this stage in the framework include considering all aspects of a teacher's planning and the different activities and methods teachers choose (or may want to choose) as they attempt to put theory into practice.

Practice: Reflecting on practice begins with an examination of our observable actions while we are teaching as well as our students' reactions (or non-reactions) during our lessons. Of course, such reflections are directly related to and influenced by our reflections on our theory at the previous level and on our principles and philosophy. At this stage in the framework, teachers can reflect while they are teaching a lesson (reflection-in-action), after they teach a lesson (reflection-on-action), or before they teach a lesson (reflection-for-action). When teachers engage in reflection-in-action they attempt to consciously stand back while they are teaching as they monitor and adjust to various circumstances that are happening within the lesson. When teachers engage in reflection-on-action they examine what happened in a lesson after the event has taken place and this is a more delayed type of reflection than the former. When teachers engage in reflection-for-action they reflect before anything has taken place and attempt to anticipate what may happen and account or prepare for this before they conduct the lesson.

Beyond practice: The final level of the framework entails teachers reflecting beyond practice. This is sometimes called critical reflection and involves exploring and examining the moral, political, and social issues that impact a teacher's practice both inside and outside the classroom. Critical reflection moves the teacher beyond practice and links practice more closely to the broader socio-political as well as affective/moral issues that impact practice. Such a critical focus on reflections also includes teachers examining the moral aspect of practice and the moral values and judgments that impact practice.

The framework can be navigated in three different ways: theory-into-(beyond) practice, (beyond) practice-into-theory, or a single stage application (I outline in more detail how teachers can reflect at each level of the framework again in chapter 5). Thus it is a descriptive rather than a prescriptive framework. Teachers can take a deductive approach to reflecting on practice by moving from theory-into-practice or from stage 1, philosophy, through the different stages to stage 5, beyond practice. Some may say that pre-service teachers who do not have much classroom experience would be best suited to take such an approach because they can first work on their overall philosophical approach to teaching English to speakers of other languages and work their way through the different stages of principles (2) and theory (3) so that when they reach the practicum stage, they will be well placed then to reflect on their practice (4) and eventually move beyond practice (5). This theory-driven approach to practice where philosophy and theory have an initial influence on practice is probably a natural sequence of development for novice teachers because they do not have much teaching experience. When their early practices are observed, it is most likely that theory can be detected in their practice; however, over time, and with reflection, it is possible that their everyday practice will begin to inform and even change their philosophy and theory and they may come up with new principles of practice. Thus continued reflection can nourish both practice and theory of practice.

Experienced teachers too can also choose to begin their reflections at level 1, philosophy, especially if they consider their philosophy as a significant basis of their practice, with principles second, theory third, and so on through the framework. For experienced teachers, some of whose practice can be theory-driven if they have been reading and experimenting with applications of particular theories throughout their teaching careers, most likely describe their work in terms of their overall philosophical approach to teaching English to speakers of other languages and this description probably embeds a lot of their values, beliefs, principles, and well as theories behind their practice. When such teachers are observed teaching their lessons, we are likely to see that their approaches, methods, and activities often reflect the influence of these theories.

Reflective Break

- What is your understanding of Farrell's (2015b) new model of reflection?
- What are the differences between his early and more recent models of reflection?
- Go through each of Farrell's (2015b) five stages as you reflect on a recent teaching experience and write your responses in a journal.
- What do you think the characteristics of an authentic reflection model may look like?

Impact of Different Definitions, Levels, and Approaches on Reflective Practice

Now that I have presented many of the different typologies/approaches to RP above and in the previous chapter concerning the different levels of reflection, it is important to consider their impact on developments in RP over the years. Because the two most influential and most cited scholars on RP are John Dewey and Donald Schön, I will begin with an analysis of their impact not only on the field but also on my own work as I feel I am standing on the shoulders of giants when I cite them and talk about their wonderful contributions to our understanding of this complex topic. I will also include the impact of the other typologies where appropriate throughout this discussion.

John Dewey is widely acknowledged as the founder of the reflective practice movement in modern times and he considered RP as an intentional, systematic inquiry that was disciplined and that would ultimately lead to change and professional growth for teachers (reflection-*on*-action). Donald Schön built on Dewey's work and added to this the idea of a practitioner being able to reflect on his or her intuitive knowledge while engaged in the action of teaching (or reflecting-*in*-action). We can also add the idea that both types of reflection: *in* and *on* action, can encourage teachers to reflect *for* action.

Dewey's and Schön's legacies are important because they moved the concept of reflection far beyond everyday simple wonderings about a situation to a more rigorous form of thinking where a teacher systematically investigates a perceived 'problem' in order to discover a solution. That said, Dewey (1933) did not consider a problem as an error or a mistake but rather a puzzling, curious, inviting, and engaging issue for a teacher to investigate. Like Dewey, I consider reflective practice as a form of systematic inquiry that is rigorous and disciplined; and like Schön, I am interested in how teachers 'think on their feet' or how they reflect in action, on action, and for action.

The implication of both Dewey's and Schön's work is that RP is considered to be evidence-based thinking, rather than obvious thinking (or as some have called it, navel gazing), where teachers should collect information or evidence (which can be called data) about their work, and then reflect on this evidence to make more informed decisions about their practice based on the evidence. Engaging in evidence-based RP allows teachers to articulate to themselves (and others) what they do, how they do it, why they do it, and what the impact of their teaching is on student learning. We can also see that many of the current typologies of reflective practice take practitioners through a similar trajectory of questions, even as simply as in Borton's (1970) questions: *what, now what, so what?* The results of engaging in such reflective practice may mean an affirmation of current practices or making changes; however these changes will not be based on impulse, tradition, or the like, but on analysis of concrete evidence.

In addition, the work of both Dewey and Schön suggests that teachers can look at what is actual and occurring (theories-in-use) in their practice and compare this to their beliefs (espoused theories) about learning and teaching. This *productive tension* (Donald Freeman, personal communication) between 'espoused theories' and 'theories-in-use' provide teachers with the opportunity to examine their practice so that they can deepen their understanding of what they do and thus gain new insights about their students, their teaching, and themselves. As Dewey (1933: 87) noted, growth comes from a 'reconstruction of experience', and by reflecting on these experiences we can reconstruct our own approaches to teaching.

Both of these wonderful scholars have had immense influence on my work and especially the development of my new typology or framework for reflecting on practice (Farrell, 2015b). Specifically from Schön's work, I was attracted to the idea of teachers reflecting while they are teaching and how this would fit into an overall model of RP, because I was also interested in how teachers 'know' through their practice and also realized that they 'know' more about their practice than they can articulate. Thus I was interested in taking Schön's pragmatic approach into the TESOL classroom and over the years have attempted to facilitate teachers as they reflected on what they think they do (their beliefs) and what they actually do (their practices) while they are teaching (e.g., most recently: Farrell & Kennedy, 2019; Farrell & Yang, 2017; Farrell & Vos, 2018; Farrell & Jacobs (2016); Farrell & Mom, 2015; Farrell & Ives, 2015; Farrell & Bennis, 2013; Farrell, 2014).

I also appreciate the typologies by other excellent scholars presented in this chapter and they have all influenced my work in many different ways. David Kolb's learning cycle for example is influential in that he focuses on the practice and can guide teachers in a systematic way on how to examine the success of their lessons and to seek improvement as a result of such reflections. While I agree with this approach somewhat and include many of these elements in my own current framework, Kolb does not take the teacher-as-person into consideration in terms of his or her identity and the impact of social and political elements on such reflections. However, his work was further developed by Graham Gibbs within the field of nursing to help with the professional development of its practitioners, and he included the practitioner's emotions while reflecting. This is a positive addition to the typologies of reflective practice because there is a consideration of the practitioner's feelings while reflecting on a particular experience and I agree with this; however, I would bring it further and include an emotional/affective aspect of reflection beyond just reflecting on a particular event or experience to include critical reflection on all aspects of our work. In other words, my framework for reflecting on practice includes such critical reflection as I believe our philosophy, principles, and theory have a huge impact on our practice and vice versa, and so RP must go beyond the narrow focus of retrospective reflections that only look at what works or does not work.

I agree with Chris Johns' idea that reflection is 'a way of being' and as such, teachers can reflect naturally during their careers. That said, I do not believe that teachers should engage each day in intensive reflections as this would be too much and would probably have a negative effect on their students' learning. Rather I believe that teaching experience should be interspersed with periods of reflection throughout a teacher's career so that they do not plateau (see Farrell, 2014). In that manner and similar to what Johns has noted, reflective practice can become a way of life for a teacher both professionally and personally.

I also agree with Stephen Brookfield's idea of critical lenses as these give us more insight into what we as individuals could be unwittingly blocking from our 'vision' about what we do. It is not always easy to look at ourselves professionally and very difficult to look at ourselves personally. When we ask colleagues to help us look, we can develop a sense of community (see chapter 6 for more on cultivating RP in communities) and when we ask our students about our teaching, we are getting them to engage in reflective learning. All this is a win-win outcome for everyone involved in the community.

As can be seen, my new framework for reflecting on practice (Farrell, 2015b) has included many elements from all of the typologies (and more not covered in this chapter) as they are useful for structuring reflection especially for novice teachers. That said, I suggest that in themselves many are too narrow and one-dimensional and do not take into consideration the inner life of the practitioner who is reflecting. The resurgence of RP in the 1980s, influenced by the wonderful scholars covered in this chapter, was against such a narrow view of teaching, or technical rationality as it was known as then. We need to guard against reducing RP to a tool to 'fix' perceived problems in teaching and thus end up developing technical teachers who take a mechanical view towards teaching and learning that some administrators may even encourage and admire. We would also end up with a different set of checklists designed to 'measure' these reflections so that they fulfil expectations set by others and not the teacher. Engaging in reflective practice should not result in technical rational teachers; rather it should result in integrated teachers because they have knowledge of who they are (their *philosophy*), why they do what they do (their *principles*), what they want to do (their *theory*), how they do it (their *practice*), and what it all means to them within their community (beyond *practice*).

Reflective Break

- What is your understanding of all the different typologies of reflection presented in this chapter?
- Which one (if any) would you choose now that you have read the chapter and why?

Conclusion

This chapter has outlined and discussed various important typologies of reflective practice so that teachers can understand the underlying traditions and theories associated with each. Understanding such typologies will give teachers more information about different structural processes that guide reflection. The main idea is not to say which typology is best; rather teachers will have to choose which one will further their own learning and reflections in their particular context. I also outlined and discussed my own recently developed framework for reflecting on practice and how it compares with the other typologies. Again, I do not want to overly bias teachers to adopt this framework but I do want to guard them against taking a reductionist view towards reflection as a 'fix it' approach to teaching problems, as this limits the teacher and brings back technical rationality that RP was originally designed to prevent. I believe we should not separate the teacher-as-human from the act of teaching, and the contents of this book (and the series that is to come) I hope attest to this.

Chapter 3

Six Principles of Reflective Practice

Introduction

As mentioned in chapters 1 and 2, reflective practice (RP) generally means that language teachers systematically examine their philosophy, principles, theory, and practices about teaching and learning throughout their careers. In this chapter I outline and discuss six principles of reflective practice. These principles show how the important concept of RP is not just a collection of methods to 'fix' perceived problems related to teaching. Indeed, we can note that many accounts and discussions of RP in general education and TESOL suggest that teachers engage in reflection to 'fix' technical issues associated with classroom management, teaching, assessment, and the like, and this reflection is far removed from the person who is reflecting: the teacher. Thus the six principles outlined and discussed in this chapter point to the depth associated with reflection that starts with the teacher-as-person and extends into and beyond the classroom to encompass a teacher's career and life.

The six interconnected principles as illustrated in figure 3.1 are:

- *Principle 1: Reflective Practice Is Holistic*
- *Principle 2: Reflective Practice Is Evidence-Based*
- *Principle 3: Reflective Practice Involves Dialogue*
- *Principle 4: Reflective Practice Bridges Principles and Practices*
- *Principle 5: Reflective Practice Requires an Inquiring Disposition*
- *Principle 6: Reflective Practice Is a Way of Life*

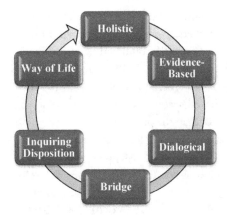

Figure 3.1 Six Principles of Reflective Practice

Principle 1: Reflective Practice Is Holistic

As mentioned in chapters 1 and 2, RP is now very popular in many professions but its definition within and across these professions can differ; however, one common notion is that reflection has often (in my opinion, too often) been represented as a tool to fix some problem or issue that has been identified in practice. Reflective practice, as the six principles in this book suggest, is more than a tool to 'fix' problems; it is a complex concept that when understood, can have great potential for language teachers to engage with their profession throughout their careers.

Although RP is not new (note Dewey's work in the mid-1930s), its relative recent resurgence can be traced to Donald Schön's work in the 1980s with the renewed interest in the concept mostly as a quest for the empowerment of teachers and out of the need to find some way to counteract an increase in teacher burnout (although Schön did not generally work with teachers) (Farrell, 2007b). Thus the renewed interest in RP in the 1980s was to counteract such burnout and as a result many different approaches and methods have blossomed since, designed to help teachers become more autonomous decision-makers both inside and outside the classroom (many of these outlined and discussed in chapter 2).

However, many approaches have since become very narrow and view reflection as a one-dimensional, intellectual exercise, reduced to a set of techniques and mainly confined to a retrospective role of questions asking teachers what they did, how they did it, and what will they do next. Yes, these are useful basic questions to help teachers to structure reflection, especially when beginning to reflect; however, the danger is that RP has now become too ritualized – and some would say mechanical and robotic – because it has been reduced to a set of prescriptive techniques for teachers to follow blindly, such as filling in recipe-following checklists as evidence of reflecting on practice (see principle 2 below for details of evidence-based reflective practice). This defeats the original purpose of the resurgence of RP in the 1980s (mentioned above) against such technical rationality where teachers are viewed as 'technicians' and where learning is assessed only by the end products rather than the processes.

The result is that in many professions including TESOL reflective practice is now something that 'gets done' (Mann & Walsh, 2013: 293) to a teacher to 'improve' some perceived weakness (a deficit approach to reflection), and as such leads to 'a real loss of reflective spirit' and a 'disregard for teacher personality' (Akbari, 2007: 201). Within TESOL, Akbari (2007: 201) has also (correctly) cautioned that, when reflection becomes a solely intellectual exercise, reduced to a set of techniques, the inner lives of teachers are overlooked and the teacher-as-person is separated from the act of reflection, and reflection is promoted narrowly as an individual, cognitive *tool* that teachers are taught to use to 'improve' their practice – meaning that there is some problem in their current practice. This type of 'reflection' adds to a teacher's burden and ultimately increases the rate of burnout because the teacher feels he or she must 'do' reflection rather than 'live' reflection (see principle 6 below). However, if we continue to ignore the inner lives of teachers, teacher burnout will continue to increase because they are not being encouraged to take the lead in their own reflection and development and as a result their students are not receiving the education they could, had their teachers been more responsive and imaginative as a result of engaging in a more holistic approach to reflection.

Holistic reflective practice focuses not only on the intellectual, cognitive, and meta-cognitive aspects of practice, but also its spiritual, moral, and emotional non-cognitive aspects; it acknowledges the inner life of a teacher and is embedded in the context of a teacher's everyday practices both inside and outside the classroom. Thus, for teachers holistic reflective practice provides a 'stance towards practice that is both affective and intellectual' (Orland-Barak, 2005: 27) that can not only lead to awareness of teaching practices but also self-awareness and understanding that equip teachers for personal and professional growth throughout their careers.

Such self-aware language teachers are more *integrated teachers* because they can understand who they are, what they do, and why they do it (see also principle 2 on evidence-based reflective practice). Such integrated teachers are contemplative practitioners because they explore their own inner-worlds through 'contemplation' (Farrell, 2015b). As Bell Hooks (1994: 13) noted, such contemplation calls for 'engaged pedagogy' because it emphasizes the notion of *well-being*: the teacher's well-being and students' well-being. In order to accomplish this openness and engagement, Hooks (1994: 15) maintains that 'teachers must be actively committed to a process of self-actualization that promotes their own well-being if they are to teach in a manner that empowers students.'

Holistic reflective practice is grounded in the belief that teachers are whole persons and teaching and reflection is multi-dimensional because it includes the moral, ethical, spiritual, and aesthetic aspects of our practice. A contemplative teacher, as Dewey (1933) has noted, stops for a moment to hit the pause button and suspends immediate judgment and decision-making when confronted with any particular issue when teaching. Such an integrated and responsive teacher slows down the interval between thought and action (or 'sleeps on it' in a manner of speaking) and engages in reflective thinking as he or she looks for alternatives rather than rushing to judgment, because this teacher has learned from experience. As Dewey (1933) noted, experience is not enough, we must learn from our experiences.

Reflective Break

- Why would some consider reflection is something that 'gets done'?
- Have you ever been stressed with the call to reflect on your practice?
- What is your understanding of an integrated teacher?
- Are you an integrated teacher?
- Do you consider your own well-being as well as your students' well-being?

Principle 2: Reflective Practice Is Evidence-Based

The second principle builds on the first. Dewey (1933) considered RP as an intentional, systematic inquiry that is disciplined and that would ultimately lead to change and professional growth for teachers. Dewey's legacy is important because he moved the concept of reflection far beyond everyday simple wonderings about a situation to a more exact form of reflective thinking whereby a teacher systematically investigates a problem in order to discover a solution. That said, Dewey did not consider a problem as an error or a mistake but rather a puzzling, curious, inviting, and engaging issue for a teacher to investigate. In this sense he encouraged teachers to make informed decisions about their teaching, decisions that are based on systematic and conscious reflections rather than fleeting thoughts about teaching or routine thinking. Dewey maintained that when teachers combined these systematic reflections with their actual teaching experiences, then they could become more aware, and this would lead to their professional development and growth. Thus Dewey was advocating early for a form of evidence-based teaching.

Reflective Break

- What is the difference between a teacher thinking about how a class went after the class without collecting evidence, and a teacher collecting evidence about how a class went and then considering how it went?
- How can a teacher collect evidence about his or her teaching?

Like Dewey, I too consider RP as a form of systematic inquiry that is rigorous and disciplined. In order to be clear about what we reflect on, we need 'evidence' to inform our decision-making and to understand what we do rather than what we think we do. I have found over the years that what teachers say they do, and what they think they do, are not the same. With an evidence-based approach to reflective practice, teachers collect data about their work and then reflect on this to make informed decisions about their practice. For example, if a teacher says he or she has had a bad or a good class, my question is: How do you know, or Where is the evidence? If the teacher replies that he or she has noticed that students looked bored or were yawing, I would ask: How we can be sure that this look or yawn has anything to do with your teaching, as the students may be tired or may have had a bad class previous to this particular one. So it is important to collect evidence from different sources.

Engaging in evidence-based reflective practice enables teachers to articulate to themselves (and others) what they do, how they do it, why they do it, and what the impact of their teaching is on student learning. The results of engaging in such reflective practice may mean an affirmation of current practices or making changes, but these changes will not be based on impulse, tradition, or the like; they will emerge as a result of analysis of concrete evidence. Evidence-based reflective practice is centered on five important questions teachers ask themselves about their practice. By systematically collecting data to answer these questions, they can engage in evidence-based reflective practice. The five questions are:

1. *What do I do?*
2. *How do I do it?*
3. *Why do I do it?*
4. *What is the result?*
5. *Will I change anything based on the answers to the above questions?*

What Do I Do?

One way of beginning is to reflect on a recent teaching practice or experience that happened in the classroom that caused the teacher to stop and think about his or her teaching for a moment or longer. For example, teachers may have experienced something that occurred in class (either positive or negative) that they had not planned or even anticipated, but they clearly remember it after class and even weeks after the incident. A teacher, for instance, can make a sudden change in the lesson plan during a class because he or she perceives that the lesson may be going better than anticipated, e.g., the teacher decides to continue with an activity until the end of the lesson because of the overall positive effect of increased student response to the activity. Conversely, something may happen in a lesson that can be problematic or puzzles the teacher into doing something he or she would not normally do, such as abandoning a particular activity or disciplining a student. The main point is that for the teacher the incident is a significant one. By recalling, describing, and analyzing such incidents teachers can begin to explore their deeply held assumptions about effective teaching practices.

Reflective Break

- Describe any one issue that you would be interested in exploring related to your teaching. This may be a incident that has gone well or not so well.
- Why did you choose this to focus on?
- Now describe the issue in as much detail as you can.
- Describe how the issue relates to your own teaching beliefs and values.

How Do I Do It?

To answer this question a teacher must collect evidence about teaching rather than just thinking about what he or she does. Teachers can gather evidence from many sources: apart from self-reflection, they can get their students' views as well as their colleagues' reflections. The point here is that teachers must cast a wide net when getting this evidence so as not to be biased in what they want to explore.

Teachers can self-reflect of course and this should be the starting point of RP. This aspect of self-reflecting leads also from principle 1 above where teachers first consider themselves as individuals in terms of their cultural, ethnic, social, and educational backgrounds as well as their life experiences as they reflect on their personal biography and how this has shaped or is shaped by their professional identity. Teachers can also self-reflect on their theory of practice (how they plan), their actual teaching practice, and where they fit within the profession (or critical reflection).

Certain reflective tools can help teachers in self-reflection and these include the use of teaching journals, and the recording of their lessons (see chapter 4 for details). Teaching journals are a good way to begin self-reflection as they provide teachers with a written record of various aspects of their practice. The very act of writing means that the teacher must slow his or her thoughts and step back for a moment to think about his or her practice. When teachers write regularly in a teaching journal, they can accumulate information that on later review, interpretation, and reflection can assist them in gaining a deeper understanding of their work (Farrell, 2007b, 2015b). Teachers who are beginning to reflect on their work without any particular focus can write regularly for a period of time, and in response to such prompts as 'What did you notice in your classes today or this week?' and 'What professional issues are of interest to you today or this week?' they can look for patterns and then after a month or so decide on a focus for their reflections. Or they may have already decided on a focus or issue and write only about this. Either way, it is important to write regularly (possibly after each lesson initially) so that you can describe your reactions (and those of your students), feelings, and thoughts at that time, because one may become too selective later in what one may want to remember. In addition, the internet these days offers more scope for teachers to share their teaching journals on a wider scale. A new approach to journal writing is keeping *online teaching journals* and *blogs* (I return to writing as a tool for reflection in chapter 4).

Reflective Break

- Focus on a recent issue you found important in your teaching. This can be something that worked well for you or did not work at all.
- Write about this issue for a few weeks as you observe how it works (or does not work) in other classes. Did you find any patterns emerging from your writing?
- What interpretations do you make from these patterns and what do these mean to you as a teacher?

Teachers can also record (audio and/or video) their lessons as an aid to self-reflection. When teachers record classes, they can get a more accurate picture of what actually happened during the lesson because it is nearly impossible for them to be aware of everything that occurs while they are teaching. When teachers are in the middle of the class, they are monitoring their students, making decisions about what they will say, and thinking ahead about where they want the lesson to go. In fact, many teachers report that they are on autopilot while teaching and find it difficult to remember exactly what happened even minutes after the lesson. But when lessons are recorded, teachers can play these back and listen for (and watch, in case of video) how much teacher talk they engage in and compare this to their lesson objectives. If they notice that they talk more than their students, while the lesson objective was to get the students talking, then they have evidence to indicate that they should make a change for the following lesson. In addition, teachers can use the recordings to explore how many questions they ask, what type of questions they ask and favor, what instructions they give, how they give them and their students' reactions to these instructions, and how they give feedback and their students' reactions to such feedback. Video recordings can show a teacher's action zone (who the teacher interacts with most and where the teacher usually stands/sits in class) as well as show what the students are doing in the class. In fact, the list of what teachers can review from a recording (audio or video) is endless. All of these are difficult to monitor while a teacher is teaching a class but can be reviewed later for reflection (see also classroom observation in chapter 4).

Reflective Break

- Record one of your classes and play it back. What do you notice first?
- What issues did you see (or hear) that you would like to reflect on further?
- Watch the video of that same class with a colleague and discuss what you see.
- What are the main differences between what you see and what your colleagues sees?

Another source from which teachers can obtain data about their teaching is their students. They can use the more traditional end-of-term student evaluations, or they can make use of concept maps. In many schools today administrators have built-in end-of-semester/year student evaluations where the students are asked to respond to a teacher's lessons over the course of a semester or year. Students are usually given a checklist developed by the school on which they fill in certain numbers or letters in response to set questions about the teacher, his or her teaching and the lessons. Some forms also allow for open-ended responses from the students. Teachers can also ask their students for feedback during the semester about what they think regarding particular lessons. For example, at the end of each class a teacher may ask the students what they thought the lesson was about, what was difficult for them and what was easy for them; or the teacher can ask students to keep learning journals where they regularly reflect on their lessons.

Concept maps can also be used to collect data as they show relationships between concepts in a type of network and as such are a useful indication of what students know (or don't know) about a topic. Concept mapping is an excellent reflection device for both teachers and students when gathering information about teaching and learning. For language teachers, concept maps can be used to measure cognitive change in their students as a result of taking their course or as a result of one particular lesson. For students, concept maps can be used to reflect on their learning as they show how students relate (or do not relate) new concepts to their current knowledge. Concept mapping can be used by teachers as a pre-activity for diagnostic purposes and/or as a way to get students ready for a particular topic. It can also be used during lessons as a record of what students are learning, and/or at the end of a lesson to see what concepts the students have understood in that lesson. Farrell (2007b) has suggested that in order to use concept mapping effectively, a teacher should first provide a *sample concept map* (because this technique may not be familiar to all students) and put his or her concepts of a particular topic as represented on a visual concept map into verbal thought by *thinking aloud*. Lastly, teachers can encourage their students to explore their identity as second language learners, and whether such an identity is desirable or if it has been imposed on them.

Reflective Break

- Construct a concept map about how to teach a particular language skill.
- Now get your students to construct their own concept maps of the same language skill you are teaching and compare it to what you constructed above.
- Have your students construct a concept map at the beginning of each lesson and at the end of each lesson and compare these. This way, students will be encouraged to reflect before and after each lesson.

Teachers can engage with their colleagues to collect data. For example, they can obtain a colleague's feedback about their teaching by incorporating peer observation in their teaching. Peers can decide if they want to observe each other teach and share feedback in an equal manner. Before each observation, they should meet to discuss what exactly is to be observed, the aim and goal of the observation, and possibly a task for the observer to accomplish. The peers should also agree on observation procedures or the type of instruments (quantitative, qualitative, or both) to be used during this session, and arrange a schedule for the observations. When classroom observations are carried out with a peer, teachers may be able to gain more self-knowledge about the type of teaching strategies other teachers use. Teachers can also meet as critical friends or in groups to discuss their teaching and classroom observations and provide support and feedback to each other through dialogue. See also principle 3 on dialogue.

Reflective Break

- How do you think a colleague could help you get evidence about your practice?
- Have you ever asked a colleague to help you reflect on your practice?

Why Do I Do It?

The answer to this particular question will depend a lot on the teacher's principles of practice or what he or she believes in regarding teaching and learning a second language. Once teachers have articulated their beliefs, they then look at their classroom practices to see if these beliefs remain valid or if they want to change their practices in light of their articulated beliefs. Teachers can also consider how others address similar issues and if this has an impact on what they will implement in their classrooms in the future (see also principle 4 below).

Reflective Break

- Have you ever wondered about why you teach the way you teach?

What Is the Result?

We teach with the hope that our students learn something from us. So, after we have examined a specific issue related to our practices, we can ask questions such as:

- What happened that was expected or surprising?
- What theories about teaching or personal experiences with learning are revealed in the data I have collected?
- How do these theories relate to my stated beliefs and attitudes?
- What are the consequences of my actions?
- What exactly are my students learning?

Will I Change Anything?

The final question a teacher can ask within evidence-based RP concerns action, as the teacher asks: Will I change anything based on the answers to the above questions? The answer to this question will of course depend on what the teacher has discovered as answers to the questions posed before, but the main point is that the teacher links the information gathered with whatever insights he or she has gained from the reflective process as a whole to whatever changes (if any) he or she wants to make in teaching practice. In such manner reflective professionals should be able to draw on many different sources of evidence, and use these to inform their teaching practices.

Principle 3: Reflective Practice Involves Dialogue

Principle 3 builds on principle 2 above and as Mann & Walsh (2017) maintain, an empirical, data-led approach to reflective practice that includes dialogue as one of its most crucial means for reflection is very important because it allows for clarification, questioning, and enhanced understanding that may not be possible for a teacher engaged in self-reflection. In addition, Farrell (2018a, b) has noted that reflection through dialogue, especially in groups, leads to the idea of building a community of practice because engagement in group discussions allowed the TESOL teachers to voice their ideas about various issues related to their practice, which in turn helped them feel a sense of community while they were engaged in their teacher group discussions.

Of course, teachers can engage in evidence-based RP by themselves and this is a good starting point for all teachers; however, while we are self-reflecting we may encounter issues or situations that may be unpleasant and so we may avoid these and become biased in our reflections to only topics that do not upset us. In other words, we can become biased in what we self-reflect on, so we may need to be challenged because we may become too comfortable with our teaching or because we have not asked ourselves some hard questions about what we do. As such, principle 3 suggests that reflective practice is informed by some kind of dialogue with the self, but mostly with others so that we can have a deeper understanding of ourselves as teachers. As Kumaravadivelu (2012: 95) has pointed out: 'Teaching is a reflective activity which at once shapes and is shaped by the doing of theorizing which in turn is bolstered by the collaborative process of dialogic inquiry.'

Reflective Break

- How can dialogue with others help teachers critically reflect on practice?

Reflective practice through dialogue begins with the self where a teacher engages in internal dialogue about his or her own practice. A teacher can begin this internal dialogue by telling his or her own teaching story, such as in an autobiography, which can be analyzed later for that teacher's stated or implied beliefs, assumptions, and values about teaching and learning English as a second language. By telling their stories teachers can make better sense of seemingly random experiences because they hold the inside knowledge (especially personal intuitive knowledge), expertise, and experience that is based on their accumulated years as language educators teaching in schools and classrooms. These self-reflection stories can provide a rich source of teacher-generated information that allows teachers to reflect on how they got where they are today, how they conduct practice, and the underlying assumptions, values, and beliefs that have ruled their past and current practices.

Reflective Break

- Tell your teaching story so far.
- What insight can you get from your story and where you are today as a teacher?

The dialogue with self can be expanded to include others as in a critical friendship or a group of teachers that form a teacher reflection group. For example, if a teacher wants to dialogue with a peer he or she can choose to enter a critical friendship, team teaching, and/or peer coaching whereby teachers collaborate in a two-way mode to encourage dialogue and reflection in order to improve the quality of language teaching and learning in some way.

A critical friendship is where a trusted colleague gives advice to a teacher as a friend rather than a consultant in order to develop the reflective abilities of the teacher who is conducting his or her own reflections. In this collaborative relationship, dialogue between the teacher and the 'friend' includes questioning, and even confronting, the trusted other, in order to explore teaching, while at the same time being heard in a sympathetic but constructively critical way. In this way, dialogues within the critical friendship can not only stimulate reflection but can also clarify and extend reflection beyond descriptive levels to more conceptual and critical levels. When teachers reflect at the conceptual level, they focus on the theory behind their classroom practices. At this level of reflection teachers can look into alternative practices which (depending on their students' needs) they might prefer to use based on their descriptions and analysis of their reasons for doing what they are doing. However, critical reflection, an even deeper level of reflection, encourages teachers to justify the work they do and reflect within the broader context of society; as such, they focus on the moral, ethical, and socio-political issues associated with their practices.

Team teaching is also a type of critical friendship arrangement whereby two or more teachers cooperate as equals as they take responsibility for planning, teaching, and evaluating a class, a series of classes, or a whole course. Of course, teams should realize that team teaching is just that – a team's, not two individuals', approach to planning the lessons, deciding and preparing the activities, delivering the lessons, and evaluating the effectiveness of the lessons. Peer coaching focuses specifically on the process of teaching and on how two teachers can collaborate to help one or both of them improve some aspect of their teaching through dialogue. Mostly, however, a peer coaching arrangement takes place so that the observed teacher can develop new knowledge and skills and a deeper awarness of his/her own teaching. To make the peer coaching work successfully, each participant must recognize that he or she has a specific role to follow in the relationship.

Teachers may also join a teacher reflection group either within their own institution or with teachers from other institutions. The teacher reflection group meets regularly to discuss and reflect on practice. These group discussions can act to break the sense of isolation expressed by many teachers when they talk about their teaching, and the group can also complement individual members' strengths and compensate for each member's limitations. When teachers gather in such groups it is important to allot roles to each member, focus on particular discussion topics for each meeting, and develop a non-threatening environment in which all the members gain supportive feedback from their peers. Thus, when language teachers come together in such a group, they can help each other to articulate their thoughts about their work so that they can all grow professionally together. One factor that should be addressed with these groups is time, as teachers are very busy. I have worked with several groups in Canada and they were initially worried about the time such meetings would take from their professional and personal lives, but as they began dialoging in such groups, they realized that it was turning into valuable time. As one group member recently noted: 'I admit that when we first talked about giving up my Saturday morning I felt a bit concerned about whether I had made the right choice but in the end felt it was time well spent.'

Reflective Break

- Look at the collaborative arrangements mentioned above (critical friend-ships, team teaching and peer coaching, teacher reflection groups). Which of these would work best for you and why?

Principle 4: Reflective Practice Bridges Principles and Practices

Reflective practice connects teachers' principles (philosophy, beliefs, theory) with their classroom practices. In this way the hidden parts which encompass a teacher's principles are directly linked to what we can see in the classroom or the teacher's actions while teaching (see also chapter 4). This is important because those who do not engage in teaching tend to look only at what a teacher does in the classroom without considering what goes on in the teacher's head and who that teacher is as a person. This fourth principle of RP suggests that teaching is like an iceberg because in both cases the hidden part that most do not see is in fact the largest part with the greatest impact; the top of the iceberg, corresponding to what is seen of the teacher in the classroom, is the smallest part.

As noted in chapters 1 and 2, this principle is influenced by Dewey's (1933) work which suggests that teachers should examine what is actual and occurring (theories-in-use) in their practice and compare this to their beliefs (espoused theories) about learning and teaching. As outlined in the previous three principles, RP thus recognizes the power of a teacher's philosophy, assumptions, values and beliefs, and theory of practice because these espoused theories of teaching influence the instructional judgments and decisions made in classrooms. Teachers are not just actors in a classroom, they are also thinking about what is happening all the time. However, not many language teachers are aware of their thinking processes or thoughts or espoused theories (beliefs) and to what extent their beliefs are reflected or not in their classroom practices (Farrell, 2007b, 2015b). Thus, when teachers engage in systematic reflective practice they can begin to uncover their principles, because as Knezedivc (2001: 10) has suggested, awareness of principles and practices is a necessary starting point in reflections since we cannot develop 'unless we are aware of who we are and what we do' and 'developing awareness is a process of reducing the discrepancy between what we do and what we think we do.' Once teachers have reflected on their principles, they can then examine how these are translated (or not) into actual classroom practice.

After teachers articulate their espoused theories (what teachers say they do in class), they compare these with their theories-in-use (what they actually do in class) to see if there is convergence or divergence between them. By systematically reflecting on the comparison of what we say we do (our stated principles), and what we actually do (our classroom practices), we can develop our understanding of what we want to do and accomplish in terms of our students' learning (by constructing our theories-*of*-, -*in*-, and -*for*-action). In other words, it is a good reflective exercise to state (or write in a journal) what you think you do in class. Then, record a class and/or ask a colleague to observe you teach and compare the two. To make it more specific, an example would be to state how you give instructions in class. Then take the class and refer to your recording or your colleague's observations of the instances where you give instructions, and see if what you say you do and what you actually do converge or diverge.

Some may say the core of RP involves teachers continually seeking to compare their espoused theories, or stated principles, with their theories-in-use, or their practices, so that they can ultimately construct their own theories-*of*- and -*for*-action. However, what teachers say they do (their espoused theories) and what they actually do in the classroom (their theories-*in*-action) are not always the same. Indeed, a review of recent principles research demonstrates that language teachers' belief systems do not always correspond with their classroom practices (Farrell & Vos, 2018; Farrell & Mom, 2015; Farrell & Ives, 2015; Farrell & Bennis, 2013). By systematically reflecting on the comparison of what we say we do, and what we actually do, or if there is an alignment between principles and practices, we can develop a better understanding of what we want to do (theories-*of*- and -*for*-action) in our classrooms. The point in reflecting on the alignment between principles and practices is not to suggest that one method of teaching is better than any other. Exploring principles and corresponding classroom practices can help clarify how teachers can implement any changes to their approaches to teaching and learning over time. Ultimately we are seeking to construct our own theories-*of*-, -*in*-, and -*for*-action.

In order to be able to construct our theories-*of-in-for*-action, teachers should be aware of the differences between reflecting *on*, *in* and *for* action. Teachers can reflect after, before, and during class and ideally all these moments of reflection are linked to each other as teachers reflect *on*, *in*, and *for* action. When teachers reflect after class this is called *reflection-on-action*. Reflection-on-action involves teachers reflecting on their classes after they have finished. In order to reflect on action teachers can record their classes with audio or video and review these, or they can have someone observe them as they teach and then discuss these observations. For example, if a lesson does not go so well, we want to find out the reasons why; and with equal interest, if the lesson goes well, we will want to know why it went well. Many of the activities in this book help teachers reflect after their classes and the framework that follows offers specific tools for teachers to consider when reflecting on action.

When teachers reflect before class this is called *reflection-for-action*. Reflection-for-action is a process where teachers prepare for future actions in their classes by formulating a detailed lesson plan that is based on the needs of the students and the knowledge the teacher has gained from reflecting on what happened in previous classes (Farrell, 2007b, 2015b). So reflection-for-action is proactive in nature enabling teachers to prepare for future action.

Reflection-*in*-action (Schön 1983, 1987) happens when a teacher is teaching and something occurs that 'upsets' the teaching routine. Thus, there is a sequence of moments in a process of reflection-in-action in which the practitioner attempts to solve a problem (see chapter 2 for an example of this). Many experienced teachers, for example, will notice when a class, although it may have been carefully planned (a teacher's theory), falls flat maybe because the students are not focused enough to study (e.g., they may be upset over something that happened in a previous class) and the teacher may want to take some action. Novice teachers, because they may not have built up sufficient knowledge about teaching routines, may find such action difficult to implement, but with time and experience and by reflecting on their teaching, they will be able to notice these classroom routines and changes that may occur while they are teaching, especially if they engage in systematic reflection after class. All three types of reflection are covered in this book. However, reflection-in-action is more difficult to capture because this happens when teachers reflect during class.

So by reflecting-*on-in-for*-action and comparing our articulated beliefs about teaching and learning, and then monitoring our teaching by regularly comparing our beliefs and practices, we can then begin to construct our theories-*of*- and -*for*-action. As Stanley (1998: 585) suggests, all three above are what 'reflective practitioners do when they look at their work in the moment (reflect-in-action) or in retrospect (reflect-on-action) in order to examine the reasons and beliefs underlying their actions and generate alternative actions for the future.' Indeed, throughout their careers, many language teachers have been expected to learn about their own profession not by studying their own experiences, but by studying the findings of outside experts. By engaging in lifelong RP (see principle 6), language teachers can now become producers of their own theories and knowledge that are grounded in real classrooms.

Reflective Break

- What are your ideas (e.g., memorization, practice speaking, grammar drills, etc.) about how a second language is learned?
- What are your ideas about how we should teach a second language?
- What is your role as a language teacher?
- What are the roles of your students?
- If you had the power, how would you design your ideal second language classroom?
- Look at the following three conceptions of teaching (from Zahorik, 1986) and see which classification best fits your approach to language teaching: *Science/Research*; *Theory/Values*; *Art/Craft*.

  Science/Research

  The science/research conceptions of teaching are derived from research and supported by experimentation. Here teaching is informed by a tested model of learning and if teachers learn specific acts of teaching (such as effective questioning, and effective wait-time), then they will be good teachers. Also, effective teachers are observed and their actions are documented. Effective teachers are identified by their students' high scores on tests.

  Theory/Values

  Here teaching is based on what ought to work or what is morally right to do. Reflective teaching would be an example of a values approach to teaching, as would following a learner-centered approach to teaching, because teachers value these approaches. There is no empirical research information to back up these conceptions of teaching.

  Art/Craft

  In this view, each teaching situation is different and unique and each teacher decides what to do based on his or her teaching skills and personality. The teacher does not follow any one method and chooses from a range of options.

- What is your understanding of reflection-*in*-action, reflection-*on*-action and reflection-*for*-action?
- How can reflecting on our beliefs and practices help us construct our own theories-*of*-, -*in*-, and -*for*-action?
- How can teachers become producers of their own knowledge?

Principle 5: Reflective Practice Requires an Inquiring Disposition

RP is not just a collection of tools or methods to get evidence about teaching; teachers need to have a particular disposition when reflecting. They must be willing to question everything both inside and outside the classroom that impacts their professional lives and also be willing to learn from what they find. Such an inquiring disposition requires that teachers develop particular attitudes to their reflections and according to Dewey (1933) three of these necessary attitudes are open-mindedness, responsibility, and wholeheartedness.

As Dewey suggested, open-mindedness is 'An active desire to listen to more sides than one, to give heed to facts from whatever source they come, to give full attention to alternative possibilities, to recognize the possibility of error even in the beliefs which are dearest to us' (Dewey, 1933: 29). To be open-minded as a teacher engaged in RP is very important because we really do not know what we will find as a result of our reflections and we must be ready for anything, even issues we may not want to face. Thus, how we interpret our findings will be important as our underlying principles may challenge our practice, or our practice may challenge our underlying principles. In other words, as we go digging into our practice we will be creating havoc for our comfortable, routine teaching practices that we have followed perhaps for many years. Engaging in RP is a rigorous exercise that challenges us to question most of our professional practice and remain open-minded throughout regardless of what we discover.

Some of what we discover may unearth some of our prejudices and educational and political ideologies that thus far may have remained hidden. This leads us to the second attitude or attribute associated with reflection that Dewey suggested was a prerequisite to any action: responsibility. Responsibility means careful consideration of the consequences to which an action leads; in other words, what is the impact of reflection on the learners? Intellectual responsibility, according to Dewey, means: 'To consider the consequences of a projected step; it means to be willing to adopt these consequences when they follow reasonably ... intellectual responsibility secures integrity' (Dewey, 1933: 30). Other scholars take this attitude further and include moral, ethical, and political issues that should also be considered so that teachers are responsible enough to develop a reflective social awareness.

Wholeheartedness, Dewey's third attitude, suggests that teachers should enthusiastically and continuously examine what they do throughout their careers. As Dewey (1933: 30) maintained: 'There is no greater enemy of effective thinking than divided interest. ... A genuine enthusiasm is an attitude that operates as an intellectual force. When a person is absorbed, the subject carries him on.' Wholeheartedness implies that teachers can overcome fears and uncertainties to critically evaluate their practice in order to make meaningful change.

Dewey added a fourth attitude that needed to be cultivated in order to engage in RP: directness. Directness implies a belief that something is worth doing, which I think nicely sums up why teachers should engage in RP: because it is worth doing. The main idea of what we do is that we teach students rather than lessons.

Engaging in RP can result in some unpleasant feelings and it is human to wish to avoid such unpleasantness. However, if teachers, as Dewey (1933) suggests, adopt a reflective disposition with open-minded, responsible and wholehearted attitudes, they will reap the vast benefits of becoming integrated and confident reflective practitioners where their students are the ultimate beneficiaries of their reflections (see chapter 6 for more details on how to cultivate such a reflective disposition).

Reflective Break

- Look at Dewey's three attributes above and see what degree of each you possess.
- What levels of these attributes do you possess as a teacher now (*high, medium, low*)?
- Which of these attributes do you need to develop more as you continue as a teacher?
- Can you think of other desirable characteristics a reflective practitioner should possess?

Principle 6: Reflective Practice Is a Way of Life

I ended chapter 1 by noting that RP is more than solving problems, it is a way of life. This supports the holistic nature of RP that I then presented in chapter 2. The sixth principle suggests that (including the other five principles) RP should not be considered just a method to explore our teaching; rather, it is more than a method, it is *a way of life*. Yes, RP requires that teachers should take a step back every now and then to systematically consider their practice(s). Teachers should be aware of what is happening in their practice throughout their careers, but also throughout the teaching day. In fact, as Oberg & Blades (1990: 179) maintain, the focus of RP is life and they suggest that 'we continually return to our place of origin, but it is not the place we left.' Thus, teachers can engage in RP at any stage of their careers and at any time of the teaching day as they continue to construct their own personal theories of teaching and improve their instructional practice.

Surely, newly graduated novice ESL/EFL teachers will wonder why, when they have just been trained and educated in all the up-to-date approaches, methods, and techniques that their particular program has just learned, there is any need to reflect on their practice. However, the call in this chapter for ongoing reflection does not mean that teachers have been inadequately trained or educated in their initial teacher education programs, but is a response to the fact that not everything a language teacher needs to know can be provided at the pre-service level (or even in in-service workshops), and also that the knowledge base of teaching is constantly changing with new theories and approaches that will need to be examined in a professional manner rather than blindly followed. Indeed, Kumaravadivelu (2003: 17) has suggested that second language teachers should enter into 'a continual process of self-reflection and self-renewal' so that they can 'construct their own personal theory of teaching.'

Teachers who engage in lifelong RP can develop a deeper understanding of their teaching, assess their professional growth, develop informed decision-making skills, and become proactive and confident in their teaching and possibly their personal life as well. RP as a way of life tends to move beyond reflecting on classroom actions to include reflection on 'who' we are as teachers, our identity, that includes the roles we play in our practice.

Teacher role identity includes teacher philosophy, beliefs, values, theory, and emotions about many aspects of teaching and being a teacher. Reflecting on teacher role identity allows language educators and teachers a useful lens into the 'who' of teaching and how teachers construct and reconstruct their views of their roles as language teachers and of themselves in relation to their peers and their context. Burns & Richards (2009: 5) have suggested that identity 'reflects how individuals see themselves and how they enact their *roles* [emphasis added] within different settings.' Teacher role identity includes how teachers recognize their roles and how these are influenced by their philosophy, beliefs, values, assumptions, and theory about teaching and being a teacher. For teachers, professional self-image is usually seen and balanced with a variety of roles that include all the functional roles a teacher uses while performing his or her duties. For example, Farrell (2011) discovered a total of 16 main role identities for experienced ESL teachers in Canada, divided into three major role identity clusters: teacher as manager (attempts to control everything that happens in classroom), teacher as professional (dedicated to their work, continuously upgrading), and teacher as 'acculturator' (helps students get accustomed to life outside class), the last of which may be somewhat unique to ESL teachers. Farrell (2011) suggests that by engaging in RP, teachers can not only become more aware of their identity roles, but also how these have been shaped over time and by whom, and how the roles need to be nurtured during a teacher's career.

Reflection as a way of everyday life is governed by our unwillingness to accept what is and to systematically question what we see in our professional practice. However, RP as a way of life means that teachers will have to possess certain qualities to enable them to constantly question their practice. As outlined in the fifth principle, Dewey (1933) identified three attributes or characteristics of reflective individuals: open-mindedness, responsibility, and wholeheartedness. We need all three as we engage in RP in order that we continue to evolve as teachers throughout our lives.

Reflective Break

- What is your understanding of the principle *Reflective practice is a way of life*?
- Which of the above three role identity clusters for a teacher's role (manager, professional, or 'acculturator') do you think best represents your role as a language teacher?
- Who has defined your role as a language teacher?

Conclusion

In this chapter I have outlined and discussed six principles of reflective practice that I think are important: *Principle 1: Reflective Practice Is Holistic*; *Principle 2: Reflective Practice Is Evidence-Based*; *Principle 3: Reflective Practice Involves Dialogue*; *Principle 4: Reflective Practice Bridges Principles and Practices*; *Principle 5: Reflective Practice Requires a Disposition to Inquiry*; *Principle 6: Reflective Practice Is a Way of Life*. No doubt there are many more I could have added but I believe these six cover the contents of this book well. I also believe these principles are related to the series that this book launches: **Reflective Practice in Language Education**. That RP is holistic, evidence-based, and dialogic, bridges principles and practice, requires a certain disposition, and is a way of life will be reflected in each of the books to come. In the chapters that follow here, I hope readers will note the presence of all six principles throughout; and at the end of reading the book, step back to see where they stand and write their own principles of reflective practice.

Chapter 4

Tools of Reflective Practice

Introduction

So far, I have outlined and discussed various typologies of reflective practice (RP) as well as six principles: that RP is holistic, evidence-based, and dialogic, and that it bridges principles and practice, requires a certain disposition, and is a way of life. When teachers engage in RP they have various reflective instruments or tools available to help facilitate their reflections. These commonly include writing, discussion, action research, classroom observations, narrative study, lesson study, critical friends, case study analysis, team teaching, and peer coaching – and online combinations of many of these. In a recent analysis of 138 journal articles on the practices that encourage TESOL teachers to reflect, Farrell (2018a) discovered that the teachers used a total of 37 different tools/instruments to facilitate their reflections with the most frequent in terms of their rate of use (it should be noted that there was some overlap that was difficult to separate) being discussion (including teacher discussion groups and post-observation conferences), followed by writing and this closely followed by classroom observations (self, peer, etc. with or without video/ audio), and then with a much lower frequency by action research. After these, the other less popular reflective instruments include narrative study and then lesson study, used infrequently. Instruments used in three or less instances included: case studies, portfolios, team teaching, peer coaching, and critical friend/incident transcript reflections. Given that there were so many different instruments used, and in the interests of space, this chapter will focus discussion on the most frequently used reflective instruments and outline what these are and how they can be used by TESOL teachers.

The following sections provide details about eight major reflective tools: dialogue, writing, classroom observations, action research, narrative study, lesson study, case study analysis, and concept mapping. A ninth important tool – portfolios – is discussed in chapter 6 in the context of teacher evaluation.

Dialogue

Teachers can come together either physically or virtually and engage in reflective discussions (see also principle 3 in chapter 3). In such discussions, language teachers systematically reflect on their practice with other teachers in a supportive environment where evaluation of comments is not entertained. These can be called teacher support groups, development groups, reflection groups, online chat groups, and so on, in which teachers come together in a mutual aid type collaboration to explore various issues that directly impact their teaching and/or their practice in general including their professional identity outside the classroom (Farrell, 2014; 2015b; Richards & Farrell, 2005). They can be informal gatherings and at the same time they can engage in small-scale projects (e.g., action research – see below) but generally membership is voluntary in nature (Farrell, 2014). Palmer (1998: 6) also noted the value of group reflection or 'the conversation of colleagues' for discussing and improving teaching. Such reflective practice groups have the capacity to discuss and then to deconstruct, analyze, and interpret critical professional events for individual members and for the group as a whole.

When language teachers come together either in pairs as in critical friends or in groups of three or more, there is no set format in terms of process or content discussed; this will depend on each group and the individual teachers who compose that group. However, research has indicated that it is best that the teachers who comprise the members share control over the process, and the best way to ensure this is to negotiate particular issues related to the group.

The first item to consider when teachers form a group for either face-to-face or virtual meetings is that they should all have a common area of interest and agree upon the general purpose/goal of the group (Farrell, 2014). Some scholars suggest that the ideal number of members in a group is between five and eight in order to make sure every teacher can participate in some manner (Farrell, 2014; Richards & Farrell, 2005). In terms of its goals, groups themselves should negotiate specific goals during their first meeting(s) but should have already established an overall set of goals before that. Each group can also decide if it wants to appoint a group leader for the entire process or to have a different leader for each meeting (Farrell, 2004; 2014). From my own experience with teacher groups, be they experienced or novice teachers, it is best to have some kind of facilitator present to manage the whole process and to ensure functioning of the group (Farrell, 2004; 2014; Richards & Farrell, 2005). Each group should have a private, safe, and comfortable place to meet that is free of distractions, and relatively convenient for all members. In terms of meeting times, this can be determined by group members while taking into account the focus of the group, the commitment of its members, and the various time constraints of its individual members.

Practicing language teachers have reported many benefits associated with engaging in group discussions, summarized as follows:

- Awareness
- Motivation
- Confidence
- Problem-solving skills
- Mutual observation/evaluation
- Mutual understanding and respect
- Connection to others leading to reduced feeling of isolation
- Emotional support
- Safe, non-judgmental and non-threatening environment
- Sharing of ideas, information and expertise
- New ways of thinking
- Empowerment and independent thinking
- Improved teaching skills
- Increasing ability to deal with classroom dilemmas
- Critical reflection
- Professional development

It has also been pointed out by many teachers that online discussions allow more time to reflect and reduce speaking anxieties, resulting in greater length and complexity of ideas discussed as compared to regular face-to-face class discussions.

There are also some challenges associated with engaging in discussions with other teachers, whether face-to-face or online. The following challenges have been pointed out by practicing language teachers as being important to address when (perhaps before) engaging in such discussions:

- Sometimes teachers do not work collaboratively
- Discussions off track
- Competing leaders
- Group commitment issues
- Online difficulties accessing the internet
- Limited access to computers
- Time factor
- Differing computing skills

Here, it has been observed that online chats are more interactive than online forums.

Although there are challenges associated with entering discussions with other teachers either in pairs or in groups, face-to-face or online, some of these issues can be alleviated when the group meets and negotiates how to avoid such challenges (see chapter 2 for ideas from my early typology on how teachers can negotiate ground rules; and Farrell, 2004). For the most part, when teachers meet to discuss practice in a supportive environment, they can voice their opinions freely on issues that are important for their professional growth as language teachers and thus develop a sense of community as a result of their membership in the group. Mann & Walsh (2017) also note the importance of dialogue as crucial for reflection as is allows for clarification, questioning, and enhanced understanding. As Ahmadi et al. (2013: 1766) noted, 'engagement in group discussions let them voice their professional identity more freely, which helped them feel a sense of community while they were engaged in group discussions.' Indeed, Hung & Yeh (2013: 163) maintained that such group discussions are very important for experienced language teachers' professional development:

> Even the teachers with many years of teaching experience still needed stimulus and support to promote their continuous learning. With facilitation for developing their practical knowledge in collaborative learning activities, they could easily extend their professional knowledge, take initiative in their own implementation, and evolve their own ongoing inquiry.

Through engaging in discussion it is likely that teachers will learn from each other because each individual teacher brings a different perspective to the discussion. Thus, discussion can result in a teacher gaining new knowledge, new perspectives, and new understandings that would have been difficult through reflecting alone. Such gatherings can generate more connections between teachers – which is important for such an isolated profession where individual teachers spend most of their day in one room (door usually closed) with different groups of students. However, when they gather in pairs or groups to discuss their practice, this isolation is reduced as teachers share their knowledge, with the result that they can all provide better learning opportunities for their students.

Reflective Break

- What is your understanding of dialogue as reflective practice?
- Do you like to talk to other teachers about your teaching? If yes, why? If no, why not?
- Which do you prefer, taking with one other teacher (pair) or with a group of teachers?
- Do you prefer online discussions or face-to-face discussions?
- What are the advantages of online discussions?
- What are the advantages of face-to-face discussions?
- What topics are important for you to talk to other teachers about and why?

Writing

Teachers do a lot of writing within their workday, be it on lesson planning, reports on students' progress or the like, but they seldom take time to write for themselves professionally about their practice. As I mentioned in chapter 1, writing has its own built-in reflective mechanism; the process entails that writers must stop to think and organize their thoughts and then decide on what to write (either using a pen or a computer). After writing they can 'see' (literally) their thoughts and reflect on these for self-understanding. This I call reflective writing and I use it all the time to help me with my own reflections.

For teachers, such reflective writing can include written accounts of their thoughts, classroom observations, assumptions, beliefs, attitudes, and experiences about their practice both inside and outside the classroom (Farrell, 2013a). Teachers can include records of critical incidents, perceived problems/issues, and insights that occurred during lessons (reflection-in-action) in order to gain new understandings of their own teacher learning and instructional practices. I actually take a notebook with me to jot down events as they happen while I teach in case I forget after the lesson – I am usually fully invested in the act of teaching during a lesson, so I cannot remember exactly what has happened after the event and I worry that I may have a selective memory. Thus, when teachers take the time to write about their practice they can express their opinions, hypothesize about their practice, and of course reflect later on what actually happened during their practice and compare results.

There are different modes of writing for reflection, some of which include teacher journals and online writing in blogs, chats, and forums. When teachers are writing as reflection on their professional practice, they can either write for themselves, or they can share what they have written. It all depends on why they write. When they write for themselves, they can include their personal thoughts and feelings as well as facts about their practice. They can read these for later reflection with the idea that they can look for patterns over time on the contents of their writing. When they reflect on the patterns they notice in their journal writing, they can become more aware of issues of interest in their practice. Teachers can also write in online formats such as blogs, chats, and forums. Such online formats are easy to use (do not require an understanding of HTML or web scripting), interactive, and can be continuously updated (Yang, 2009). Some TESOL teachers report that online writing formats are better than discussions because teachers can challenge peers online easier than when discussing issues face-to-face (Yang, 2009).

When implementing reflective writing either with traditional pen and paper, or using electronic media, it is always best to set goals for writing and choose what audience you are writing for (yourself and/or others). In addition, teachers should set a time frame for the writing activity as there is a danger it may fizzle out without such allocated time (Richards & Farrell, 2005). As noted above, it is a good idea to review entries regularly to find emerging patterns (Chien, 2013) and also evaluate the journal writing experience to see if it meets the goals that have been set (Richards & Farrell, 2005).

Teachers also must consider different types of levels of writing they can engage in. Hatton & Smith (1995: 85) identified four levels of writing.

- *Descriptive writing* (not reflective) reports events that occurred or is a report of something you have read in the literature. There is no attempt to provide reasons or justifications for the events. Its main purpose is to provide a support or a starting point for the framework.
- *Descriptive reflection* attempts to provide reasons and justifications for events or actions but in a descriptive way. Although there is some recognition of alternative viewpoints, it is mainly based upon personal judgment, e.g., *I chose this problem-solving activity because I believe the learners should be active rather than passive.*
- *Dialogic reflection* demonstrates a 'stepping back' from the events/actions leading to a different level of mulling about discourse with one's self through the exploration of possible reasons, e.g., *I became aware that a number of students did not respond to written text materials. Thinking about this, there may have been several reasons. A number of students may still have lacked some confidence in handling the level of language in the text.*

- *Critical reflection* demonstrates a level of awareness that actions and events in the classroom (and beyond) are explained by multiple perspectives. It involves giving reasons for decisions or events, which takes into account the broader historical, social, and/or political contexts, e.g., *What must be recognized, however, is that the issues of student management experienced with this class can only be understood within the wider structural locations of power relationships established between teachers and students in schools as social institutions based upon the principle of control.*

Teachers can choose to structure their writing in a kind of developmental sequence from the non-reflective, descriptive writing to descriptive reflection, becoming more able to give a range of reasons for acting as they do. Then they can take a more exploratory examination of why things occur the way they do, and engage in dialogic reflection. Finally, as Hatton & Smith (1995) note, teachers can take a more critical perspective depending on where they are reflectively.

Many practicing language teachers have reported benefits associated with engaging in writing as reflection, summarized as follows:

- Increased awareness
- Self-evaluation
- Deeper understanding of classroom practices and events
- Recognition of patterns
- Connection and integration of ideas
- Prepares student teachers for the complex realities of teaching
- New insights about teaching
- Promotes changes in teachers' beliefs
- Improves teaching skills
- Promotes reflection
- Can be used collaboratively
- Professional development

There are also some challenges associated with writing as reflection, whether in traditional or online modes. The following challenges have been pointed out by practicing language teachers as being important to address when (perhaps before) engaging in such writing:

- Adds to teachers' workload
- Demanding: thorough preparation is required for writing journals
- Peer feedback not clear
- Protectionism (concealment of information about oneself or others)
- Manipulation of information (faking it)

- Reflections more descriptive than critical
- Discomfort with critical reflections and critical responses for fear of damaging friendships
- Time management (making time to blog)
- Struggle to extend the reach of blog

Some of these issues can be alleviated before teachers begin their writing. Overall reports from TESOL teachers suggest that reflective writing can help teachers become more aware of their beliefs and practices about language learning and teaching. As Genc (2010: 407) noted for EFL teachers, 'Reflective journals guided them to criticize, build knowledge about teaching a language, and gain the autonomy to make more conscious and informed decisions about their classrooms. These decisions were based on their explorations and reflections on teaching in their classes, which represent the bottom-up view of teaching.' Genc (2010: 407) continued that teachers developed 'bottom-up teaching strategies based on the dynamics of their classrooms through critical reflection in journals because they were able to explore, analyze and observe their own beliefs and classroom practices, and experiment with alternative instructional behaviors.' Thus, by writing regularly teachers are able to identify and address issues critical to their practice within their teaching contexts, and as a result provide more learning opportunities for their students.

Reflective Break

- What is your understanding of teacher writing as reflective practice?
- Do you like to write about your teaching? If yes, why? If no, why not?
- Do you like to share your writing with other teachers?
- Do you prefer online writing or writing in your journal (computer or paper)?
- What are the advantages of online writing?
- What are the advantages of writing in your journal (computer or paper)?
- What topics are important for you to write about and why?

Classroom Observations

Teachers can systematically reflect on their practice through classroom observations of what they do while they teach. These can be conducted either alone, with a facilitator, supervisor, mentor, or with peers. When teachers engage in classroom observations to reflect on their teaching they generally want to see if what they say they do (their beliefs) is what they actually do (their practice) and generally hope that there is more convergence between the two, rather than too much divergence. Thus they must decide if they want to capture a broad picture of their lessons in a descriptive manner as a means of uncovering patterns in their actual teaching behaviors, or to capture a narrow picture of a particular lesson by focusing on specific and/or pre-determined behaviors such as teacher questions, instructions, wait-time, and so on.

Teachers have a variety of instruments at their disposal to collect data about their teaching while engaged in classroom observations. They can for example decide to take a general approach to collecting data by using such instruments as written ethnography (Richards & Farrell, 2005) and/or they can record their lesson by audio and/or video recording (Day, 2013; Farrell, 2011). Teachers can also take a more detailed approach by using some form of category instrument to collect data, such as checklists (Richards & Farrell, 2005) or even a particular category instrument such as SCORE (seating chart observation record) (Farrell, 2011).

As mentioned above, teachers can use the above instruments alone while reflecting on their teaching or they can get assistance from others who will observe them as they teach. Regardless of where they come from, it is best that the observers are trained in some manner in how to watch, listen, and record (but not take active part in) the lesson. Day (2013) for example suggested that when peers engage in observation during a practicum, it is best to conduct this in four stages: pre-observation conference, observation, post-observation conference, and peer observation report.

Regardless of the focus of the observation or the instruments used to collect data, teachers can use classroom observations as a means of examining and analyzing teaching events as part of their overall reflections on their work. Many practicing language teachers have reported benefits associated with engaging in classroom observations, summarized as follows:

- Provides direct evidence of classroom behavior
- Large amounts of descriptive data can be collected
- Increases ability to evaluate own teaching practices
- Promotes change towards more effective teaching strategies
- Aids novice teachers in conceptualizing what goes on in the L2 classroom
- Promotes self-exploration
- Promotes self-awareness
- Increases collegiality
- Promotes reflection about specific (rather than imagined) teaching practices
- Promotes professional development

There are also some challenges associated with engaging in classroom observations either alone or with others. The following challenges have been pointed
out by practicing language teachers as being important to address when (perhaps
before) engaging in such observations:

- Time-consuming
- Presence of observer has an effect on (and hence alters) the situation being
  observed
- Induces anxiety, particularly when the observer is a master teacher or
  administrator
- Colleagues may avoid providing constructive feedback if they fear that it
  may offend the observed
- Observers, if supervisors, may exercise top-down authority

Although there are challenges associated with engaging in classroom observations either alone or with others, some of these issues can be considered before
the observations so as to avoid such challenges. For the most part, when teachers engage in classroom observations in a supportive environment, they can better examine what they do rather than what they think they do because they have
obtained evidence from whatever instruments they have used to collect this evidence. For example, Farrell (2011) reported on a short series of classroom observations where a facilitator for a novice ESL teacher used a seating chart observation
record or SCORE as a category instrument to collect hard evidence and discovered
that such a non-inferential classroom observation instrument was most beneficial
to novice ESL teachers than more open-ended instruments because it enabled the
teacher to move from a descriptive reflective phase to a more critical stance on her
practice. The instrument allowed the teacher to see that there was convergence
between her stated beliefs and her actual classroom practices.

Thus, when teachers engage in classroom observations using a variety of feedback sources such as listening to audio recordings and/or watching videos of their
teaching, they can develop increased awareness regarding their teaching and their
students' learning. Such raised awareness of their teaching behaviors and their
impact on their students' learning can lead to more focus on their students' needs
and how to respond to these needs so that they can provide the best possible learning opportunities for their students.

The main reason for classroom observations is for teachers to develop such
awareness, rather than have others judge them for what they perceive of the 'best'
way to teach. One immediate problem with evaluating teachers on 'good teaching'
is that there is still no agreement on what 'good' means in all situations. Many
times, then, 'good' is based on preconceived opinions that may (or may not) be

based on the most up-to-date development in research associated with the latest methods and approaches. For example, I have had the opportunity to observe teachers in schools worldwide that still favor behaviorism and teacher-centered/controlled lessons; however, these same teachers are being trained in up-to-date developments that include more learner-centered approaches that are not considered 'good' by their supervisors. Classroom observations should be developmental in that teachers can learn more about what they actually do (rather than what they think they do), and consider now that they have this information, whether they want to change anything as a result.

Reflective Break

- What is your understanding of classroom observation as reflective practice?
- What do you think when some supervisor or colleague says they would like to observe you teach? Are you happy or worried?
- Do you like to share your classroom observations with other teachers?
- Do you prefer audio-recorded lessons, video-recorded lessons, or peer observations of your lessons?
- What are the advantages of audio-recording lessons?
- What are the advantages of video-recording lessons?
- What are the advantages of peer observations of your lessons?
- What would you most like to learn about in your teaching from being observed by peers or supervisors?
- What topics are important for you to observe and why?

Action Research

Action research and reflective teaching practice are depicted as closely connected because action research comes under the umbrella of reflection. Action research has been defined variously and there are many forms, arising from different epistemological bases. It is best to dissect the two words and examine them as two components: *action* and *research*. Looking at the latter word first, we can say that *research* means some kind of systematic collection of information or data in a planned manner (some may say planned interventions), followed by some form of analysis of what is revealed by the information or data, a formal reflection on the implications of these findings for possible further observation, and then action (Farrell, 2018a, b). The *action* component can be seen as a process of planned interventions in which concrete strategies, processes, or activities are developed within the research context discussed above (Farrell, 2018b). Thus, putting the two components together we have action research through which teachers examine various issues in their classroom teaching with the idea of changing their practice in some way in order to improve their teaching. Or as McFee (1993) points out, action research is the investigation of those craft-knowledge values of teaching that hold in place our habits when we are teaching and it concerns the transformation of research into action. As McFee (1993: 178) says: 'It is research into (1) a particular kind of practice – one in which there is a craft-knowledge, and (2) is research based on a particular model of knowledge and research with action as an outcome ... this knowledge is practical knowledge.'

Thus, action research for language teachers suggests that it serves to address and find solutions to particular problems in a teaching and learning situation, and so it is undertaken to bring about change and improvement to a particular teaching practice. What the many different definitions of action research all have in common is that it involves inquiring into one's own practice through a cyclical process that includes planning, acting, observing, and reflecting (Kemmis & McTaggart, 1988).

The general stages (cyclical) of the action research process are (Farrell, 2018b):

- Plan (problem identification)
- Research (literature review)
- Observe (collecting data)
- Reflect (analysis)
- Act (redefining the problem)

The language teacher sees a need to investigate a problem (perceived or otherwise) and then starts to plan how to investigate ways of solving this problem. The teacher starts reading some background literature on the problem to give him/her ideas on how to solve the problem. Of course, this 'research' cycle can include talking to other colleagues about the concern as they may have some advice to offer. The teacher then plans a strategy to collect data now that the problem has been identified and researched. Once the data has been collected, the teacher then analyzes and reflects on it and makes a data-driven decision to take some action. The final step in this spiraling cycle of research and action is problem redefinition. In this way, language teachers can take more responsibility for the decisions they make in their classes. However, these decisions are now informed decisions, not just based on feelings or impulse.

Practicing language teachers have reported many benefits associated with engaging in action research, summarized as follows:

- Improved self-efficacy
- Supports student teacher development
- Better understanding of own students
- Develops an inquiry stance
- Stimulates and promotes reflection on practice
- Promotes reflective learning
- More open to new and varied strategies
- Changes in teaching practices
- Changes in beliefs
- Changes in understanding of teaching, identity, and educational discourse
- Deeper awareness and understanding of own classroom practices
- Improved research skills
- Improved confidence in practices
- Improved theory-practice connections; relationship between action research and the classroom

There are also some challenges associated with engaging in action research and language. Teachers quickly realize that each action research project will demand a high level of commitment (especially related to time) in order to go through each level or stage, otherwise the 'research' will not have the impact they would have liked in enabling them to provide more opportunities for their students to learn. The following challenges have been pointed out by practicing language teachers as being important to address when (perhaps before) engaging in any action research project:

- Heavy workload
- Teachers have limited research skills
- Particular methodological decisions within the action research project need support from others more experienced in action research
- [But] other instructors already too overworked to help
- Lack of financial support
- Teachers face contextual obstacles: time constraints, lack of collegial support, and a rigid curriculum
- Action research is a challenging process

Although there are challenges associated with action research, especially when conducting such a project alone, some of these issues can be alleviated when the research is undertaken with other like-minded teachers. This process is sometimes called collaborative action research and such studies have reported positive effects for all the teachers concerned as well as their students (Banegas et al., 2013).

Action research is a form of self-reflection inquiry when conducted alone and group-reflection when conducted collaboratively. It occurs within a social context and addresses concerns for teachers in their classrooms within the contexts in which they work. By engaging in action research projects as part of their reflections on practice, language teachers can re-examine their philosophy, assumptions, beliefs, and theory as they decide on action plans put in place to improve their practice. However, teachers must be on guard against the notion that action research is a 'fix-it' approach to RP, separating the teacher from the act of teaching as they try to solve a perceived problem in their practice. Teachers must be on guard against entering such an 'action research bubble' and becoming obsessed with change rather than self-understanding; and action research must be grounded in the complete cycle of RP which encourages understanding of the self. As Dewey (1933) noted, teachers must slow down to think and not rush in to do or change. Parker J. Palmer (1998: 3) put it best when he said that good teaching cannot be reduced to a technique that the language teaching industry is so guilty of promoting over the years; 'good teaching requires self-knowledge.' Thus, when language teachers engage in action research either alone or collaboratively, they are seeking not only to improve their practice but also to gain self-knowledge. As Palmer (1998: 3) understood it: 'whatever self-knowledge we attain as teachers will serve our students and our scholarship well.'

Reflective Break

- What is your understanding of action research as reflective practice?
- Have you ever conducted an action research project?
- Why do you think action research is not a 'fix-it' approach to reflective practice?
- Why is it important to include the teacher-as-person or self-understanding when conducting an action research project rather than just looking at the 'problem' that needs to be 'fixed'?
- What topics are important for you to engage in action research and why?

Narratives

Teachers can reflect on work by telling the story of their experience – giving narrative accounts of life as a teacher. These teacher-generated stories offer valuable information for the teachers themselves because they are usually emotionally driven and can be infused with interpretation. Such teacher narratives serve to bring meaning to teachers' experiences and as such offers them more evidence of who they are, where they came from, and who they want to be professionally (Farrell, 2015b). I have used narrative analysis as I reflected on my own professional role identity (Farrell, 2017). I was interested in exploring my concept of 'self' (or the *who* as in 'who I am is how I teach') as an essential consideration of my identity so I could better align my philosophy, principles, and theory with my practices and beyond practices. I believe whatever self-knowledge we attain as teachers will serve our students and our scholarship well because we will be centered as human beings while still professionals.

Teacher narratives reveal important events identified by teachers, and when articulated, different events can be linked, patterns observed, and coherency developed between these events. In such a manner meaning is made by narrative analysis. Thus teachers can use the interpretations made from their narratives of events to bridge the theory/practice gap that often exists . Teachers can engage in personal theorizing as a result of telling their story as each event in their experience has a particular meaning for them.

Teachers can just tell or write the story of their professional lives or they can use some scaffolds such as narrative frames for more structure when telling their stories. They can simply tell and/or write their life experiences in chronological order or they can write an in-depth biography that offers insights into their past to uncover their philosophy of practice, by mapping out various past experiences and how these may have been impacted by their culture, family upbringing, education, religion, community, and the various experiences that have helped shape them as individuals and as teachers. When teachers have reflected on their story, they can then consider how these past experiences have shaped their philosophy of practice, or (in the case of novice teachers) how they think it may shape their philosophy of practice.

While some teachers may be comfortable with straight storytelling, others may need to be provided with a structure for writing their narratives. This structure can be in the form of narrative frames. Barkhuizen & Wette (2008) suggest that a narrative frame is really a story template consisting of a set of incomplete sentences that teachers must complete. Such frames, they note, provide guidance and support in terms of both the structure and content of what is to be written (Barkhuizen & Wette, 2008).

Telling one's story can be transformative for a teacher because the story reveals assumptions, values, and beliefs embedded in events that can be unraveled as the teacher theorizes about his or her practice. Practicing language teachers have reported many benefits associated with telling their story, summarized as follows:

- Offers a safe and non-judgmental environment to share the emotional stresses and isolating experiences of the classroom
- Increased understanding of teaching experience
- Increased control over thoughts and actions
- More mindful of teaching
- Promotes change to improve teaching practice
- Promotes reflection on teaching experience
- Facilitates professional/cognitive development

There are also some challenges associated with teacher narratives or teachers telling their story as RP. The following challenges have been pointed out by practicing language teachers as being important to address when (perhaps before) engaging in narrative:

- Time commitment
- Narrators selective in what they tell
- Difficult to construct the narrative
- Ethical issues
- Who interprets the story of their lives?
- Narrative frames and content structure may not be compatible with the way a particular writer would like/is able to structure his/her story
- Narrative frames tend to de-personalize the teachers' stories
- Narrative frames may be poorly designed and/or misinterpreted

Although there are challenges associated with teachers telling their stories either chronologically or within the structure of narrative frames, some of these issues can be considered more closely before telling their story. For the most part, when teachers tell their stories, they can get a better sense of 'who' they are professionally (and personally) and if necessary engage in a process of developing a new story of who they want to be as a language teacher. As a result of reflecting on their narratives, teachers become more aware of the emotional dimensions of their practice as well as of the complexity of their lives in terms of their strengths, triumphs, weaknesses, and disappointments – and how all these combine to make them 'who' they are professionally (Shelley et al., 2013). Thus, as a result of telling their stories, language teachers can gain a newfound awareness of the complexities of what shapes their practice outside lesson planning and other aspects of their theory of practice, and as a result, develop plans for future action.

Reflective Break

- What is your understanding of narrative study as reflective practice?
- Do you like to tell stories about your teaching? If yes, why? If no, why not?
- Do you like to share your stories with other teachers?
- What topics are important for you talk about in terms of your teaching story and why?
- Do you think narrative frames would be helpful for you to tell your story?
- What is your understanding of 'who I am is how I teach'?
- Is the person you are the teacher you are?

Lesson Study

Lesson study is another instrument language teachers can use to reflect on their practice. This is popular in Japan and involves language teachers working together to plan and teach various lessons. Lesson study is collaborative, teacher-directed, non-evaluative, and grounded in everyday classroom practices. In lesson study teams of teachers usually co-plan a lesson, and after the lesson, the team (the teacher, observers, and any outsiders invited) gather together to discuss their observations. After the group discussions, the team revisits the lesson based on the feedback they received and a revised lesson is then delivered either to the same class or to a different group of students. A second review is held that focuses on the overall effectiveness of the lesson. The lesson study cycle ends with the team publishing a report, which includes lesson plans, observed student behavior, teacher reflections, and a summary of the group discussions.

More recently collaborative lesson planning has evolved into two different types: product-oriented approach and problem-based approach (Xu, 2015). In a product-oriented approach to lesson study, teachers produce a complete, ready-to-use set of teaching resources as a visible product which is then shared among the team. In a problem-based approach to lesson study, teachers can co-produce discussions (may be detailed or not) on certain teaching issues, which as Xu (2015: 146) notes, may 'not provide concrete help in physical forms but may inspire insights and facilitate exchange of teaching experience.' Xu (2015: 146) maintains that 'product-oriented collaboration is more likely to alleviate novice teachers' anxiety as it contributes to a more supportive community environment, while problem-based collaboration tends to leave novice teachers with the impression that they are forced to struggle on their own, especially at the very beginning stage of their teaching careers.'

In addition, lesson planning can be conducted in online modes such as discussion boards, chat rooms, wikis, audio chats, virtual worlds, and podcasts (Dooly & Sadler, 2013). The nature of such online lesson study collaborations can be dialogic discussions of practice, and/or displays of teacher talk that enable teachers to make more theory/practice connections and promote development of critical thinking as a result of reflection on lesson study. Studies that use such online collaborative lesson study modes have reported that such teacher-teacher collaboration results in improved lessons.

Many practicing language teachers have reported benefits associated with engaging in collaborative lesson study, summarized as follows:

- Online lesson study facilitates autonomous and collaborative learning and organically accommodates individual needs in multifaceted levels
- Helps pre-service teachers experience realities of teaching before jumping into the career
- More positive impact of autonomy on teacher development
- Enables theory-practice connections
- Moves from 'knowledge telling' to 'knowledge transforming'
- Leads to internalization of nexus of practice
- Development of critical thinking
- Opportunity to produce meaning
- Opportunity to exercise agency

There are also some challenges associated with engaging in lesson study as RP. The following have been pointed out by practicing language teachers as being important to address when (perhaps before) engaging in such reflections:

- May not equip teachers with the tools they need to reflect on and question existing practices in order to develop throughout their careers
- Time factor
- Sometimes teachers do not work collaboratively
- Discussions off track
- Colleagues may avoid providing constructive feedback if they fear that it may offend the observed
- Observers, if supervisors, may exercise top-down authority

Although there are challenges associated with engaging in lesson study, some of these issues can be considered before the lessons and observations so as to avoid such challenges. For the most part, when teachers engage in lesson study in a supportive environment, they can learn how to innovate or refine a pedagogical approach as a result of the collaboration with other teachers. In addition, the results of their lesson planning can be shared with others though dissemination in seminars or conferences or publication in journals. Shi & Yang (2014) reported on the positive effects of lesson study that allowed TESOL teachers to exchange their views openly, and thus to develop a shared understanding while at the same time negotiating their own views on their practice. Lesson study allows such collaboration with other teachers in order for all concerned to have a better understanding of their practice.

Reflective Break

- What is your understanding of lesson study as reflective practice?
- What are the advantages of lesson study over the other tools already outlined above?
- What is your understanding of the differences between a product-oriented approach and problem-based approach to lesson study?
- Which approach would you like to follow?
- What topics are important for you within lesson study and why?

Case Analysis

Another useful tool for exploring practice is to reflect on case studies related to that practice. Case studies are factual accounts of what teachers actually experience in their practice. They are usually developed by teachers and outline and discuss various issues related to practice. They offer insider information about how teachers have dealt with events in their professional lives. When teachers construct case studies, they outline real-life teaching events which can be pulled apart for further analysis by other teachers as a means of uncovering their own theory of practice.

Cases may be subject-specific or context-specific. For example, cases can give detailed accounts of dilemmas of practice that can occur within a lesson such as a problematic classroom routine or activity, or a learner discipline problem. Cases can also focus on a teaching activity such as a writing activity or a speaking activity, or can be more focused on issues of how to set up activities and/or deal with transitions between activities. The main point is, when a case is deconstructed through a process of questioning and analyzing, teachers can become more aware of how their theory may have influenced how they acted in a particular situation and consider whether they want to continue to hold the theory or not (Farrell & Baecher, 2017).

Cases can be constructed specifically for use in teacher education programs so that they are designed to stimulate discussion and reflection (Richards & Farrell, 2005). Cases can take many forms such as narratives (see above), journal entries (see writing above), and/or video/audio of teaching (see classroom observations above). The main point is that cases can provide teachers an opportunity to reflect on, as Shulman (1992: xiv) has observed, '[t]he messy world of practice, where principles often appear to conflict with one another and no simple solution is possible,' and then make their own judgments about what has occurred from their perspective and from within their context. Thus preparing, reading, and discussing cases provides information about teaching that is produced by teachers themselves and addresses their own real needs and issues.

The following are examples of case studies that could be used as part of a teacher reflection activity (from Richards & Farrell, 2005: 128–129).

- Information collected over a period of a semester concerning how two different students (one with high proficiency and one with low proficiency) performed during group activities
- An account of the problems a teacher experienced during her first few months of teaching
- An account of how two teachers implemented a team teaching strategy and the difficulties they encountered
- An account of observation of one high-achieving student and one low-achieving student over a semester in order to compare their patterns of classroom participation
- A teacher's journal account of all of the classroom management problems she had to deal with in a typical school week
- An account of how a teacher made use of lesson plans over a three-week period
- An account of how two teachers resolved a misunderstanding that occurred between them in relation to the goals of a course
- A description of all the changes a student made in a composition she was working on

Wassermann (1993) has suggested that cases be processed by teachers in three different stages. The first stage is fact-finding where teachers generate questions about relevant facts in order to surface all of the details that are possible clues for later analysis. This is followed by meaning-making where all the information from the previous stage is organized to make sense of it by identifying the problems within the case. The final stage is problem-solving where teachers attempt to make decisions about the case based on the previous set of information.

Many practicing language teachers have reported benefits associated with analyzing and reflecting on case studies, summarized as follows:

- Promotes problem-solving and decision-making
- Enhances knowledge and understanding
- Reflection in and on action
- Provides basis for arriving at valuable insights and principles
- Allows teachers to share their problem-solving strategies
- Promotes collaboration
- Increases pre-service teachers' awareness of unfamiliar settings and of their own values and beliefs
- Narrows the gap between theoretical knowledge and practice
- Sharpens overall communication skills

There are also some challenges associated with constructing and analyzing case studies. The following challenges have been pointed out by practicing language teachers as being important to address when (perhaps before) engaging in such analysis:

- Too descriptive
- Too theory-driven and not enough of real-life teaching
- Not enough detail
- Important facts omitted
- Underlying issues missing
- Does not clearly identify for whom the issue is a problem

Although there are challenges associated with constructing and analyzing case studies, some of these issues can be alleviated before teachers begin their construction and analysis. Overall reports from TESOL teachers suggest that reflecting on case studies can help teachers become more realistic about the real world of teaching because they provide vivid details about what teachers actually experience from their frames of reference. When teachers analyze case studies they learn how to frame problems because they can identify important issues related to their own practice. As a result, they develop more awareness of the teaching-learning complexities that exist and quickly realize that there are no simple solutions or answers.

Reflective Break

- What is your understanding of case analysis as reflective practice?
- Have you ever created a case about any aspect of your practice?
- What topics are important for you to compose as a case and why?

Concept Maps

The construction and analysis of concept maps is another good tool in facilitating language teachers' reflective practice. Concept mapping allows language teachers to have a visual of the concepts they 'see' as being important for them regarding their beliefs and practices. As a result, teachers can reflect on how these maps represent their underlying philosophy, beliefs, theory, and practices. Concept maps can reveal beliefs and concepts formed in previous learning and life experiences, and through reflection, teachers can begin to understand particular concepts and relationships among those concepts that are now represented graphically (Farrell, 2009). Concept maps can also be used to track conceptual development over time and they illustrate that the length of teaching experience is not an adequate predictor of teacher effectiveness (Mergendoller & Sacks, 1994).

Language teachers can also use concept maps with their second language students, for example, at the beginning of a new lesson in order to gauge how much their students have learned from previous lessons and/or to discuss any misunderstandings that may have occurred about the content of previous lessons. Zaid (1995) has maintained that teachers can use concept mapping within a lesson in three places. Concept mapping can be used by teachers as pre-activity for diagnostic purposes and/or as a way to get students ready for a particular topic. They can also have students use concept maps during lessons as a record of what they are learning and teachers can later look at these maps to see if both are on the same track. Finally, teachers can use concept maps as a post-assignment in lessons to see how their students understood concepts presented in the lessons.

The process of concept mapping can take any format but the following process with statements as its main focus has been recommended by different scholars:

- Preparation (selecting the participants; developing the focus)
- Generation of statements (brainstorming)
- Structuring of statements (sorting of statements; rating of statements)
- Representation of statements (computation of maps)
- Interpretation of maps
- Utilization of maps
- Planning (action plans; planning group structure; needs assessment; program development)
- Evaluation (program development; measurement; sampling; outcome assessment)

Many practicing language teachers have reported benefits associated with concept mapping, summarized as follows:

- Evaluates what teachers (especially novice teachers) know about teaching
- Tracks conceptual development over time
- Tracks conceptual change before and after taking a course
- Tracks conceptual differences between novice and expert teachers
- Increases teacher awareness
- Raises awareness of prior beliefs
- Increases group cohesiveness and morale

There are also some challenges associated with concept mapping. The following challenges have been pointed out by practicing language teachers as being important to address when (perhaps before) engaging in concept mapping:

- Elicits implicit groupings of ideas only
- Difficult for novice teachers to critically interrogate their own assumptions and beliefs about language teaching
- Concept mapping is complicated
- Maps difficult for teachers to interpret
- Process only descriptive and not critical
- Difficult to make clear connections to identity formation

Although there are challenges associated with concept mapping, some of these issues can be alleviated when the group meets and negotiates how to avoid such challenges. For the most part, when teachers construct, analyze, and reflect on concept maps in a supportive environment, they can assist teachers to develop awareness about their philosophy, principles, theories, and practice and how these develop over time. Farrell (2009) outlines how the mapping process helped a teacher educator to evaluate both what pre-service teachers know and how they conceptualize it as a representation of their cognitive processing, and how this led to critical reflection. Farrell (2009) sees the process of concept mapping as a way of revealing beliefs and concepts formed in previous learning and life experiences, among these being second language teacher education (SLTE) programs. The mapping exercise in a SLTE course elicits pre-service teachers' expectations about the coming course, and thus provides the tutor with valuable insights into the assumptions and beliefs they bring to the program. The increasing sophistication of pre-service teachers' thinking as the course progresses is also visible in their maps, and it is significant that the early representations are, to some extent, residues of previous SLTE courses (among other early experiences) followed by participants. Thus concept mapping for both teachers and students is a useful tool to facilitate reflecting on teaching and learning.

Reflective Break

- What is your understanding of concept mapping as reflective practice?
- Have you ever created a concept map about any aspect of your practice?
- What topics are important for you to compose as a concept map and why?
- Teachers can use concept mapping within a lesson in three places: as pre-activity for diagnostic purposes, during lessons as a record of what they are learning, and as a post-assignment in lessons. Try using all three concept maps in your next lesson and see how useful they are for the purposes of reflection.

Conclusion

This chapter has outlined and discussed various tools that can be used by language teachers to facilitate their reflections on their practice. The chapter provided details about the benefits and challenges of using such tools as dialogue (including online dialogues), writing, classroom observations, action research, narrative study, lesson study, case analysis, and concept mapping to aid teachers as they reflect on their practice. Not all these tools are used with the same frequency by teachers but they are presented in the order of frequency used as outlined by Farrell (2018a) in his analysis of 138 journal articles on the practices that encourage TESOL teachers to reflect on their practice. It is also possible to use many of these tools/instruments in combination to aid RP, as for example in online reflections where teachers may want to write their dialogues and then decide to partake in an action research project on some focus of these 'discussions' and so on. I would imagine that teachers will not use any one tool exclusively but rather in combination, within their preference for one particular tool over another. As this book is the inaugural book in the Equinox series on reflective practice for language education, I am hoping that many of the above reflective tools will be discussed in more detail in individual books to come, to facilitate language teachers reflect on their practice.

Chapter 5

One Teacher's Reflective Journey

Introduction

Chapters 1–4 have outlined and discussed various definitions, levels, typologies, principles, and tools of reflective practice (RP). As also mentioned previously, scholars within the field of teaching English to speakers of other languages (TESOL), just as in the field of general education, have struggled to come to a consensus as to how RP should be operationalized. There are many different approaches suggesting a retrospective mode of questioning about practice. As a result, many of these approaches have led to a type of routinization of reflection. Worried about such routinization, I have developed a more holistic approach to reflective practice that recognizes the spiritual, moral, and emotional aspects of reflection as well as the usual retrospective questions about practice (Farrell, 2015b). Such a holistic and comprehensive model for RP must include an examination of not only the technical aspects of one's practice, but also the internal aspects (i.e., the teacher's philosophy, principles, and theory), as well as the external aspects (i.e., the social, cultural, and political settings in which one teaches); I call this the *framework for reflecting on practice* for TESOL teachers (Farrell, 2015b).

As we have seen, the framework for reflecting on practice has five different stages (or levels) of reflection: *philosophy*; *principles*; *theory*; *practice*; and *beyond practice*. The framework is summarized as follows: Philosophy explores the 'teacher-as-person' and suggests that professional practice, both inside and outside the classroom, is invariably guided by a teacher's basic philosophy and that this philosophy has been developed since birth. Principles include reflections on teachers' assumptions, beliefs, and conceptions of teaching and learning. Theory explores and examines the different choices teachers make about particular skills taught (or which they think should be taught) – in other words, how they put their theories into practice. At the practice stage, teachers reflect while they are teaching a lesson (reflection-in-action), and after they teach a lesson (reflection-on-action). The fifth and final stage, beyond practice, takes on a socio-cultural dimension to teaching and learning, and entails exploring and examining the moral, political, and social issues that impact a teacher's practice both inside and outside the classroom. As Farrell (2015b: 25) suggests, when teachers reflect about their own lives and how 'their past experiences may have shaped the construction and development of their basic philosophy of practice, they will then be able to reflect critically on their practice because they will become more mindful and self-aware.' Thus Farrell's (2015b) framework suggests that reflective practice includes several elements such as a cognitive and intellectual dimension to ensure that it is a systematic way of thinking to promote rigor, but it also includes an affective and personal dimension that embraces the person-as-teacher who reflects in terms of his or her desires, expectations, goals, motivations, and personality.

This chapter outlines a case study (from Farrell & Kennedy, 2019) of the reflective practice of an experienced TESOL teacher in South Korea using the framework in Farrell (2015b). Subsequently, using many of the reflective tools outlined in the previous chapter, we explore in detail the reflections of this teacher (called Richard, a pseudonym) on his philosophy, principles, theory, practice, and critical reflection.

Richard's Reflective Journey

Richard, an African-American male teacher of English as a foreign language (EFL), was working in a public English Experience Center in rural South Korea. He held a Bachelor of Arts in Communication at the time of the study and was in the process of acquiring his teaching license through correspondence for teaching English as a second language in the US. At the time of his reflections, Richard had just begun his eighth year of teaching in public schools in South Korea.

South Korea's push toward greater communicative proficiency in English has prompted some local governments to establish so-called English villages and camps where students stay for a number of days and are expected to use English throughout their experience. The same group of students may only be taught for a limited period once or twice a year at a camp. As an *English Experience Center*, Richard's school represents one variation of such English camps where students (typically elementary level) come from various locations within the county to take part in an intensive immersion program over two days. To maximize exposure to English, these schools provide all the students' meals and sleeping arrangements, and teachers are strongly discouraged from speaking Korean when students are present. Lessons taught in accordance with school mandates emphasize English as an experience and tend to follow a typical task-based language teaching (TBLT) format beginning with schema activation, controlled practice, a focus on linguistic elements, and freer practice before having the students perform a pedagogical task. Pedagogical tasks are performed with the use of specialized theme rooms. Much like film sets, these rooms are decorated to give students a more immersive experience and include such settings as a post office, an airplane, a hotel, a bank, a store, and a kitchen. Although teachers are expected to make effective use of these theme rooms, the schools do not implement an official curriculum. The English Experience Center where Richard was a teacher catered to elementary level Korean students of English. Both foreign and Korean English teachers work at this school; however, at the time of this study, only the foreign teachers were teaching classes.

Data were collected over a month-long period and included interview data, classroom audio-recordings, and Richard's written reflections. Richard's reflection was facilitated by following the steps outlined in Farrell's (2015b) framework for RP. A total of six interviews were conducted for this study via internet video-conferencing. These included one pre-interview in which Richard's basic information was collected before beginning his reflections, and five post-assignment reflection interviews: one for each of the five stages of Farrell's (2015b) framework. All the interviews were audio-recorded and transcribed. Data were also collected through audio-recordings of four lessons over a span of one week. These recordings too were transcribed.

Richard's Philosophy

This section reports on Richard's reflections on his philosophy of practice, in which five identity traits emerged as having the potential to impact his practice. These aspects appeared to have evolved one from the other, following a chronological progression from his early childhood up to, and including, his career as a teacher. As outlined in table 5.1, all these aspects can be traced to memorable events or experiences in Richard's life.

Born in Long Island, NY where he spent his early childhood, Richard recalled being very shy during this phase of his life, stating, 'I was a very quiet child. I didn't enjoy talking to strangers as I perceived them. That included people related to me.' Richard soon learned to cope with his shyness, however, when at the age of five he moved to North Carolina, where he began attending school and established a core group of neighborhood friends. He described this period of his life as being rather average, up to the time of his parents' divorce when he was an adolescent. While challenging, this next part of his life also proved formative by instilling in Richard a sense that transience was a normal part of life. Within two years, Richard had

Table 5.1 Richard's Philosophy

Personality Trait	Sources
Shyness	Early childhood in New York
Ability to make friends	Moving to North Carolina
Transience as a normal part of life	Parents' divorce Moving within North Carolina Multiple schools Socio-cultural transitions
Value of education and new experiences	Family values Personal goals
Value of setting achievable goals	Family values Personal goals
Desire to satisfy his curiosity	Decision to live and work to South Korea
Rewarded by providing students with new experiences	Career

attended three different middle schools and had lived in three different homes. Describing an especially jarring transition in which he had to deal with an entirely new socio-cultural environment, Richard reported:

> I went from growing up in a suburban neighborhood that was mostly middle class and mostly white to going to middle school in an urban area that was completely black. [...] And, I did make friends, it was just weird. I would say that had my friends from the first school had a chance to meet the friends from the second and vice versa, they probably would have been okay.

Richard's discussions of his over-achieving sister, and his mother's perseverance in getting Richard into a better funded and better staffed high school, indicated that education was valued in his family. However, Richard never felt pressured to surpass his sister's successes. Rather, what seemed to be more important was that he set achievable goals and pursued them to completion, as evidenced both by his mother's insistence that he graduate from high school and college, and by his motivation to pursue a career in education.

Eventually, these values developed into the sense of curiosity and self-improvement that would prompt Richard to try teaching abroad. When asked what he had thought working abroad could offer him, Richard responded by saying:

I thought that I could get a chance to see more of the world. [...] So, I felt like it was pretty obvious that there's no better way to do that than to take a job overseas, someplace else, and I thought that teaching English ... everything that I had read and learned online about it seemed like, 'Oh this is a fairly simple thing, and you kind of get to train as you go along.'

When asked if he had achieved his intended goals, he replied, 'Not only is this something that's unique and special, and I feel good doing it, but I feel like I'm getting better doing it, and I enjoy doing it, and so I've just kept doing it.' Thus, teaching English abroad not only satisfied Richard's curiosity, it also allowed him to build a rewarding career.

Regarding Richard's in-service experience, a sense of curiosity was also something he came to foster in his own students. In his written work and in our interview, Richard frequently referred to the rewards he obtains by providing students with new experiences. And while this may at least partly be a result of his working in a so-called English Experience Center, the importance Richard ascribed to this point cannot be overlooked. Speaking at length about the joy he feels when seeing students' reactions to a new food, Richard reported, 'I really do get a kick out of the kids cooking and then eating things and being like, "Wow! This is delicious!"' Additionally, when asked how his students or co-workers might describe him and his lessons, Richard focused exclusively on his value as a provider of new and interesting experiences.

Reflective Break

- What is your philosophy of practice?
- What has influenced your philosophy?
- What is your understanding of the EFL teacher Richard's philosophy of practice?
- Do you have anything in common with Richard?
- How does your philosophy differ?

Richard's Principles

This section reports on Richard's personally held assumptions, beliefs, and conceptions. As outlined in table 5.2, Richard's stated assumptions and beliefs appeared to fall into two categories of principles: the principle of approachability, and the

Table 5.2 Richard's Principles

Principles	Assumptions	Beliefs
Approachability	• All teachers memorize students' names • Approachable teachers make students more likely to engage in lessons • Making personal connections with students is necessary for seeing growth	• Make time to interact with students • Be active • Be fun • Exhibit a welcoming personality
Fostering curiosity	• Language is better retained when learning is interesting	• Teachers should use creative, hands-on activities • Language learning requires a mind opened through new experiences (linguistic and cultural)
Conceptions	• Making decisions based on extensive experience • Flexibility, versatility, and preparation • Accounting for individual learner needs as they are encountered (i.e., not applying the same principle to everyone)	

principle of fostering curiosity. And as conceptions are said to encompass a teacher's beliefs and practices (Farrell, 2015b), these were treated as a separate category.

Subscribing to what could be described as the principle of approachability, Richard's stated beliefs and assumptions about what makes a teacher approachable largely originated from his reflections on his own fourth grade teacher, whom he admired as a role model. While Richard described his teacher as having a fun, active, welcoming, and accommodating personality, what differentiated this teacher from all others in his mind, was his willingness to make time for interaction outside of the classroom.

Richard's sense of curiosity was also very evident in his assumptions and beliefs on the importance of fostering curiosity in his students. Specifically, Richard held the assumption that when learning is interesting, language is more likely to be retained. While Richard believed that creative, hands-on activities made valuable contributions to language lessons, he explained the importance of gaining new perspectives when learning a language:

> I think that it's important to teach them a different way to think about situations and to make them think differently than they are used to. Language shapes the way that we do so many things that we don't really think about, and it's even easier to not think about those things

when you're in elementary school and you just go along with the world thinking that it is one way.

Regarding conceptions, Richard displayed an overall guiding framework in which decisions were most often made based on his extensive teaching experience. Richard even used this to separate himself from other, less experienced co-workers when, in regard to classroom management he said:

Some of them complain like 'Ah these kids, they're so talkative,' and I think part of that is that they're fairly new teachers, but for me, I feel like I'm okay, and I can handle the kids, and keep their attention.

Richard used an interesting metaphor for a teacher when discussing his principles. He said: 'A teacher is like a Swiss army knife,' and went on to explain the meaning of this metaphor in terms of teacher flexibility with young learners: 'You have to be flexible and nimble. You can't take up too much space. You have to have lots of different tools and abilities within you, ready to spring forth at any moment, and you have to be ready.' This indicated Richard's adherence to the principle that a teacher must be flexible, versatile, and prepared for any possible situation. Moreover, Richard's use of this metaphor asserted the notion that a teacher must be ready to use different tools for different types of students, and should not rely on a one-size-fits-all approach.

Reflective Break

- What is your understanding of Richard's metaphor, A teacher is like a Swiss army knife?
- What is your metaphor for an ESL teacher: A teacher is like a __?
- What are your beliefs about teaching and learning?

Richard's Theory

Richard's reflections on his theory were divided into two parts: his teaching methodology, and his planning procedures. In terms of methodology, Richard made a distinction between what he considered task-based approaches, and more traditional structural approaches. For Richard, a task-based approach was defined not only by the existence of a problem to be solved, but also by the degree of teacher intervention in solving this problem. In fact, it was the proportion of teacher-led guidance, in Richard's view, which determined whether an approach would be deemed task-based or structural. While Richard had great appreciation for the emotional connection students make with the language when performing hands-on tasks, he admitted that he feels more comfortable when taking a more traditional structural approach, because it is the most familiar to him. Despite his stated proclivity for more structural approaches, Richard also revealed a strong liking for physical, student-centered activities when recounting his experiences teaching a handball-themed lesson in which students were forced to initiate communication with Richard in English in order to appeal a ruling he had made which they did not agree with.

Regarding planning for lessons, Richard reported that he prefers not to be bound by extensive plans, and that outside of the worksheets he has created, he does not follow a textbook. He stated that while he must abide by the directives of his supervisors, their only expectation is that he uses the theme rooms effectively. When planning lessons, Richard stated that he usually considers the level of the students with the task level and then he tries to 'come up with an activity to build the lesson around if it is the kind of situation that benefits from action.' This indicated that Richard's primary concerns when planning are the activities that will be used, and whether they are appropriate for the students and the theme of the room.

Reflective Break

- How do you plan your lessons?
- What is your understanding of forward, central, and backward planning?
- Give examples of how you use each of these.

Richard's Practice

Richard recorded four lessons; class 3 (G3) and class 4 (G4) were each taught one airplane-themed lesson (A) and one cooking-themed lesson (C). Airplane-themed lessons for both classes included a role play as the main activity. Cooking-themed lessons, on the other hand, included a hands-on pizza making activity for class 3 and an ice-pop making activity for class 4. Table 5.3 provides a summary of the practices that were observed (O) or not (N) in these lessons.

As shown in table 5.3, all four of Richard's recorded lessons featured the instruction of new vocabulary, accounting for at least half of the instructional time in each. When teaching vocabulary, Richard primarily selected lexical items that students would need to perform the major activity, although new, culturally specific terms were also introduced. Typically, Richard followed a procedure in which a lexical

Table 5.3 Richard's Practice

Observed Practices	G3: C	G4: C	G3: A	G4: A
Teacher introduced new vocabulary	O	O	O	O
Teacher drilled pronunciation	O	O	O	O
Teacher provided students with a new experience	O	O	O	O
Teacher incorporated cultural information into the lesson	O	O	N	N
Teacher diverged from original lesson plan	O	O	O	O
Teacher accommodated students' unique traits	O	O	O	O
Teacher made himself available to students	O	O	O	O
Teacher included hands-on activities in the lesson	O	O	N	N
Teacher engaged in informal interactions with students	O	O	O	O
Teacher exhibited a fun, active, and welcoming personality	O	O	O	O
Activities motivated students to practice speaking	O	O	O	O
Question Types				
Total questions asked	68	120	160	177
Referential questions	10	6	19	7
Display questions	20	12	25	21
Reformulated questions	2	7	7	9
Comprehension checking questions	20	33	17	24
Wait-time: Amount of silence between when a question was posed and an utterance was made — < 1 second	19	37	159	27
1 second	12	15	21	15
2 seconds	2	11	18	3
3 seconds	1	4	7	1
4 seconds	1	0	5	1
> 4 seconds	3	0	7	1
Elicitation Types				
Confirm: Elicits confirmation that students are able or ready to perform a task	3	13	22	5
Inform: Elicits information from students	18	49	42	21
Repeat: Elicits repetition from students; occurring most frequently during listen and repeat task sequences	29	25	68	19
Agree: Elicits agreement from students	1	0	0	1
Commit: Requests that students perform a particular task	0	0	8	6
Cluing: Elicits a correct response from students by providing only partial information	1	55	23	4
Corrections: Teacher elicits the correct form in response to incorrect student utterances	0	4	12	0
Withholding information: Negative evaluations given to elicit new responses	0	1	3	1

item was introduced using pictures displayed on a screen. The English word and occasionally its Korean translation would then be elicited, followed by pronunciation drills. Richard often reported that what students were most likely to take from his lessons was a new set of English words. However, Richard also felt that students always left his class with a new experience, even if they learned nothing else. Richard's cooking-themed lessons achieved this goal by introducing students to various international foods, while airplane-themed lessons allowed students to interact with themes they were unlikely to encounter at their regular schools.

Notably, all of Richard's recorded lessons diverged in some way from the original lesson plans that accompanied them. In our discussions, Richard revealed that most of his quick decisions to make changes, either by cutting out or re-ordering activities, were in consideration of his students' abilities. For example, in Richard's third airplane-themed lesson, he diverged from his original plan of having each student perform each role in a dialogue, by instead having each student perform only one of the roles while he read out the other. Although he had made this decision in consideration of his students' abilities, Richard expressed regret that he had not done more in advance to accommodate lower-level students. When asked what he would have altered, Richard stated, 'I would tone down the control tower dialogue. Or, streamline it, is probably a better way to put it, because then it's easier reading for the students of all levels.' Richard went on to say that had the dialogue been simpler from the beginning, students would have had time to practice both roles instead of just one. This was one of many examples demonstrating Richard's constant concern for creating and using activities that would match students' abilities.

During individual and group activities, Richard maintained a fun, active personality resulting in an atmosphere in which the students felt free to engage in informal interactions with the teacher. This was exemplified by an amusing exchange which took place as Richard was preparing the ice-pop making activity for the fourth graders:

Excerpt 1

T: [eating a gummy bear] Mmm.
S1: Oh! One, please!
T: You can have a smell.
S1: [smelling the bag of gummy bears] Mmm! Ah! Teacher!
S2: Teacher, where is the cider? Teacher! Where is the soda?
T: It's in the refrigerator. Where do you think it is?
Ss: Oh! Teacher!

Note: T = teacher; S# = specific student; Ss = multiple students

While these types of exchanges demonstrated Richard's efforts to create a more relaxed environment by speaking to students as he would to any of his friends, Richard distinguished between the hands-off approach he takes in these parts of his lessons, and the more traditional approach he takes when teaching vocabulary. Indeed, an obvious shift in the teacher's role could be seen to split each lesson into two parts: an initial teacher-fronted section in which Richard would primarily initiate interaction and evaluate responses; and a more student-centered activity section in which independent self-discovery was fostered. Richard explained that in the second half of his lessons, when circulating he prefers to take a 'step back' by withholding information in the hope that students will come to the right conclusions on their own, as exemplified in the following excerpt:

Excerpt 2

T: So, matching. Can you match? Draw the line. Draw a line from picture, *geulim* (picture/drawing), yes, to the word, okay?

Ss: Ah! *Algetda!* (I understand!)

[Students connect the pictures and words in their workbooks]

[Teacher circulates]

T: Oh. Can't see? Okay.

S: Teacher.

T: Mmhmm? Yeah...yes.

S1: Yes? Ah! *Yeongyeol hane yedeula!* (Oh, we need to connect, everyone!)

S2: *Ige mueoyeyo?* (What's this?)

S1: This? This? Yes?

T: Yeah.

S1: *Ah, yeongyeol haneun geo gatda!* (Ah, it seems like we need to connect!)

S2: *Ileoke.* (Like this.)

S3: *Duetda.* (Finished.)

Note: *Italics* = Romanized Korean, followed by translation in brackets; T = teacher; S = one student; Ss = multiple students; S# = specific student

This excerpt demonstrates Richard's tendency to give students time to think for themselves, all the while remaining attentive and supportive. Additionally, during more teacher-fronted portions of his lessons when students were less likely to initiate communication, Richard encouraged interaction by inserting referential questions in between display questions, as in the following excerpt taken from his fourth grade airplane-themed lesson:

Excerpt 3

T: [makes flying noise] All right. What is this?

Ss: Airplane!

T: Airplane! Good! And, have you been on an airplane?

Ss: Yeah!

T: Oh! Really? How long? How many hours? *Myeot Shigan* (how long)? How many hours?

Ss: [inaudible]

T: Ten hours? Oh my...

Ss: Eight.

T: Eight hours? Oh my...

Note: *Italics* = Romanized Korean, followed by translation in brackets; T = teacher; Ss = multiple students

Richard established his priority of ensuring all students could freely contribute when he stated that referential questions were the best questions to ask in class because they allowed students to share their own experiences in a comfortable environment. Moreover, while also highlighting his ability to read his students, this priority emerged prominently in Richard's classroom practice through a number of instances in which decisions were made in the interest of student inclusion.

Reflective Break

- Have you ever reflected on the classroom interactions in your lessons?
- If yes, how did you do this and what did you find?
- If no, what type of interactions would you be interested in looking at?
- How do you set up the seating arrangements in your classroom?
- How do you think the seating arrangements impact the classroom dynamics in your lessons?

Richard's Critical Reflections (Beyond Practice)

In this section, Richard's critical reflections will be outlined according to how Richard perceives power dynamics at the classroom, school, and socio-cultural levels.

Classroom level: When describing his relationship with his students, Richard described himself as more of a friend than a boss in most cases, although he felt that younger students may see him as more of an authority figure. Richard stated that students likely see him as a 'fun-time teacher,' which he felt was a positive outcome of working at an English center as it meant that he was making learning fun for students and providing a break from their hectic schedules. Richard contrasted his current position with his past positions, where he was seen as more of an authority figure resulting from the fact that students were being tested on the material he taught.

School level: At the school level, Richard stated that he enjoys a great deal of freedom in how he conducts his lessons. The absence of a school mandated curriculum means that once the head teacher assigns Richard his rooms, the rest is up to his own discretion. Although he is expected to submit lesson plans and materials to the head teacher, Richard stated that he is rarely asked to revise any of his work. Richard also enjoys a great deal of job security as he understands that unless significant interpersonal problems arise, the Korean teachers in charge of hiring new foreign teachers would prefer to keep their workloads to a minimum. The downside of this, according to Richard, is that the teacher evaluations conducted by those same teachers have little value, and he would prefer to get an honest assessment from teachers outside of his school, even if it meant slightly less job security.

Socio-cultural level: Richard made it apparent that a clear divide existed between the five foreign teachers and the three Korean teachers who work at his school when he described what he saw as a great discrepancy in the respective workloads of each group with the Korean teachers seemingly refusing to teach any classes at all. This discrepancy has opened a rift between the two groups as the foreign teachers have pleaded with the Korean teachers to take on some of their night classes. While two of the Korean teachers, including the head teacher, appeared to be willing to teach these classes, they said that they were prohibited from doing so by a widely followed Korean tradition that restricts teaching to the daytime. Richard attempted to explain this as follows: 'I think that the two teachers that are willing to teach are not willing to go against the cultural norms, and tell the third teacher that she just has to teach classes. It's fairly obvious that that's the problem.' As dialogue has failed to bring about a resolution to this problem, Richard foresees job action to be the next logical step, stating, 'Ultimately, I think that they will have to do what we request, because if they don't, we are not contractually obligated to do these classes. We are getting paid for them, but we don't have to do them. We are getting paid over time for them, so we could say "no".' While overall it appeared that Richard enjoys the freedom of working in an English center, his critical reflection revealed that there are factors which he feels unfairly affect his workload and his ability to grow as a teacher.

Evaluation

Themes which emerged in the findings detailed above indicated that the aspects of Richard's reflection, i.e., his philosophy, principles, theory, practice, and critical reflections, are all linked to and mutually influenced by each other. While the themes to be discussed emerged in all aspects of Richard's reflection, they did so in different ways in each stage, indicating that each reflective stage provided a different lens through which to view the factors that influenced Richard's practice.

Approachability

The first theme which could be seen to link each stage of Richard's reflection was that of approachability. Emerging throughout his reflective journey, Richard displayed a strong attachment to this notion, beginning with the events that shaped his philosophy. Frequent relocations throughout his childhood taught Richard how to recognize and appreciate approachable people, as indicated by his prediction that his two groups of friends 'would have gotten along pretty well' despite their vastly different backgrounds. These values fed into his teaching, and thus his principles, as he affirmed his assumption that being approachable allowed even the most apprehensive students to engage in class. Richard's assumptions and beliefs regarding approachability could then be seen to inform his theory as Richard embraced the roles that activity-based lessons provided: allowing students to initiate interactions, and allowing Richard to play the role of facilitator rather than transmitter of knowledge. This was evident in Richard's classroom practice, as one excerpt from the third grade pizza-making activity exhibits:

Excerpt 4
Ss: Finish!
T: All right. Now, have some basil.
S: Basil?
T: Basil, yeah. Sprinkle this on your pizza. [distributes basil]
     [Students top their pizzas with basil, chattering in Korean]

T: Hm. Yes.
    [1-minute pause: students complete their tasks]
Ss: Finish!
T: Finished? Oh! Haha! All right, I will put it in the oven. If you want, you
    can go and wash your hands.
S: Okay!
Note: T = teacher; S = one student; Ss = multiple students

What else is evident in this excerpt is that instead of evaluating his students' responses, Richard replied to his students' initiations: indicating that their contributions were valued (Farrell, 2004). While Richard's lessons still tended to rely on teacher-led communication patterns, his use of referential questions as presented in Excerpt 3 helped to maintain approachability in situations where conversation would be otherwise one-sided. Stating that referential questions allow students to think for themselves about what the teacher is asking and how they want to answer, Richard indicated that he follows a constructivist model which, according to Farrell (2004), entails seeing students as active participants who filter information through their own belief systems.

Flowing into his critical reflections, Richard's strict adherence to his principles of approachability likely influenced his sense of maintaining an egalitarian power structure in his class. Emphasizing his intention of providing students with a relaxed learning environment, Richard embraced the idea of having less authority, and prioritized giving students a good impression. Thus, Richard's sense of approachability grew out of his own experiences and into his practice via his principles, theory, and perspectives of the social dynamics within the classroom.

Art-Oriented Conceptions

According to Zahoric's (1986) three-part classification of teacher conceptions, teachers with *science*-oriented conceptions of language teaching are guided by research and experimentation, while *theory*-oriented teachers use reasoning to make decisions on what ought to work in most cases, and *art*-oriented teachers use personal experience and skill rather than any particular teaching method to analyze classroom situations and select appropriate courses of action. Using this classification, the present study's findings revealed that Richard subscribed to an art-oriented conceptual framework and this framework, like Richard's sense of approachability, was apparent in all aspects of his reflection.

As part of Richard's philosophy, art-oriented conceptions influenced how Richard saw himself in relation to others as indicated by his differentiation of himself from his co-workers in terms of his ability to draw on his experience when managing classes. As these conceptions appeared to run as deep as his own perceptions of himself as a teacher, these philosophies transferred into Richard's principles, as evidenced by his frequent references to his teaching experience when making decisions, and his beliefs that good teachers are flexible and able to account for learner needs as they are encountered.

It was also evident that Richard drew upon these beliefs in constructing his theory. When asked how he would teach a lesson on prepositions with little advanced notice, Richard justified his choice of certain activities by stating, 'I have quite a bit of experience teaching prepositions to third or fourth graders so I have a wealth of knowledge to pull from, personally, of what works and what doesn't work with certain age groups.' Additionally, Richard's tendency to use more traditional teacher-led communication patterns during instructional phases may also be linked to his reliance on teaching experience. As Richard explained, 'A bit of it is [that I'm] trained that way. But, I think a lot of it is ... I've just done it so much more during my time teaching.' Art-oriented conceptions also surfaced in Richard's theory through his planning procedures which appeared to draw from the activities to be used rather than the content, or the outcomes to be expected. This indicated that Richard follows what has been described as a central planning design (Farrell, 2015b), with which parallels can be drawn with art-oriented conceptions. As activities developed through a central planning design are done according to the teacher's interpretation of the educational context, as well as the teacher's expertise in creating materials and managing instructional processes, it can be inferred that such a planning design would be well-suited for a teacher whose principles align with art-oriented conceptions.

As was described in a previous section, Richard's school is such that the same group of students may only be taught once or twice a year. Richard frequently discussed this aspect of his work environment in negative terms, and referred to his inability to witness students' growth, and the difficulty of predicting students' proficiency levels as 'painful.' As art-oriented teachers perceive the range of options at their disposal according to their analysis of the educational context in which they work, Richard's seeming preoccupation with student proficiency was not surprising. However, aligning with this study's findings in which modifications to original lesson plans were an expected component of Richard's practice, it has been found that more experienced teachers tend to diverge from lesson plans when pedagogical factors, like a need to simplify tasks or to provide more focused language work, prompt on-the-spot modifications. Thus, while Richard appeared critical of having to constantly cope with unpredictable classroom situations, his art-oriented conceptions explain his appreciation for the freedom in planning and teaching he was afforded at this center, as it allowed him to make the quick decisions he felt were necessary.

Curiosity

Like the last two themes discussed, the notion of fostering curiosity in students recurred frequently throughout Richard's reflections although in slightly different forms at different stages. Reflecting on the events that shaped his philosophy, Richard revealed the factors which encouraged his *own* sense of curiosity to grow (i.e., comfort in the unknown, a family who pushed him to pursue new goals, and a desire to see the world). As a principle, however, curiosity became not only something to be had, but something to be *shared*, as Richard explained, 'I think that one of my *main* responsibilities is to foster curiosity in English and help it grow through the years that I have the chances.' As this statement demonstrates, Richard not only saw fostering curiosity as his duty, but as an opportunity not to be squandered.

When viewed in terms of Richard's theory, fostering curiosity in students by way of providing new experiences became a tool for language teaching. Through the course of his reflections, Richard's formula for fostering curiosity emerged wherein new and positive experiences introduced through stories, games, cooking, and other activities, prompted student engagement, attention, and interest. A by-product of this engagement reported by Richard was that higher-level students, excited by what they were experiencing, would translate for their lower-level peers, thus creating more engagement. Another by-product frequently mentioned by Richard is that students would remember their experience and crave more similar experiences, thus starting students down what he hoped would be a path of continued English education.

Curiosity transferred into Richard's practice as his objective of providing students with new experiences was observed in all of his lessons, and most evidently in the cooking-themed lessons. In these lessons, Richard's efforts to foster curiosity were most visible in hands-on activities. However, it was also evident that Richard's choice of target vocabulary was dictated by these same objectives. For instance, in the fourth grade ice-pop making lesson, vocabulary instruction included a component on international snacks, while the third grade pizza-making lesson introduced various pizza styles and their origins. While perhaps not as overt, Richard's choice of vocabulary coupled with role plays, allowed him to inject experiential learning into his airplane-themed lessons as well. As Richard explained, 'I want students to understand some language they might hear on an airplane before take-off. If they hear "seatbelt" hopefully it is something that sticks for them.'

Going beyond his practice, as Richard works at a so-called English Experience Center, there is an obvious impetus for all teachers at Richard's school to provide new experiences to students. So much so, as Richard reported, that language instruction may be viewed as an objective of secondary importance. With this in mind, it is entirely possible that what appears to be Richard's own predilection for fostering curiosity may in fact be what Brookfield (1995) refers to as a *hegemonic assumption*, i.e., an assumption which is perceived by teachers as something worth working diligently to uphold, when in reality it has been manufactured by higher powers to maintain the status quo. While Richard's critical reflection did not provide any data to indicate he thought this to be the case, it might be speculated that another result would have emerged had Richard started his reflective journey by looking beyond his practice.

As these themes indicate, Richard's philosophy, principles, theory, and critical reflections appear to flow, one from the other, influencing his classroom practice. However, this apparent convergence does not imply that the same insights could have been arrived at had Richard reflected on only one aspect (e.g., principles) in isolation. Rather, the results of this case study speak to the utility of a multi-dimensional approach to teacher reflection, as it allows teachers to see how what is uncovered in one stage may have been influenced by the preceding stage, and vice-versa. Moreover, while one may progress through the stages of reflection in a linear fashion as in this study, the recursive nature of Farrell's (2015b) framework allows teachers to see how even seemingly distant aspects interact as critical reflection may influence philosophy and theory may influence principles, and so on. Therefore, rather than as a straight line, these results show that reflection is better viewed as a wheel in which philosophy, principles, theory, and critical reflection interact with each other as spokes connected through the hub that is our practice.

This case study also demonstrates the contributions that various modes of data collection can have in exploring teachers' philosophy, principles, theory, practice, and critical reflection. As such, this study is intended to encourage teachers to reflect using the means at their disposal so as to become more aware of the technical, internal, and external aspects of their practice in developing their own approaches to teaching. While it was not the intention of this study to promote any particular 'best practices,' the information it provided was meant to allow Richard to make informed decisions and to develop strategies to change what he himself deems necessary (Farrell, 2007b). It was evident that these intentions were met when, in a follow-up conversation, Richard commented on his comprehension-checking practices stating, 'I know that I can change these and I look forward to making myself better with this information.' Thus, by engaging in evidence-based, systematic reflection teachers can come to their own conclusions about what they feel needs to be improved to provide the best learning environment for their students, as exemplified by Richard's conclusion that 'I don't want to inhibit my students by overloading them with language and I need to be more aware of that in the heat of the moment in class.'

Richard's Meta-Reflections

Richard's overall self-assessment of his reflective journey is also illuminating and this is presented in his own words as he reflects on what he read in the evaluation above. In his own words:

Looking back at it now this is a really nice summation of what I feel has made me the teacher I am. Someone that is a bit curious and shy at the same time. I'm not sure that I would change anything in my current position. Being at an English Experience Center instead of a regular Elementary School really requires thinking about classes in terms of what can you expose them to, in 40 minutes, instead of what you can build on from yesterday or last week that a teacher in a normal position might do.

My Philosophy

I think there is something in me that, when I was younger and all these things were happening around me, part of me learned to say just go with it, make sure that you try and take something out of each life event or lesson, large or small, that you have going on. So I can see me wanting to make each lesson for the students something that is at least a little memorable for them. If I can do that every lesson is a success in my mind.

My Principles

This is a good summarization of my principles. Being open to students as well as flexible and prepared for anything to happen in the classroom is the cornerstone of being able to teach elementary school, especially so in Korea, where things tend to happen and change quickly. If you are open and available to students then you will hopefully be able to foster a greater understanding. The students might respect what you say more and be willing to listen to you a little more than if you were just a new teacher with a stern face or a quiet teacher they don't get to interact with. I think this is just human nature though; we smile at people we like and know.

Flexibility with individual students lets you extract the maximum out of each classroom interaction. Forcing a student to try and read a paragraph when you know that they have no reading skills is not going to improve their situation or move your class along. If anything you will frustrate, anger, and embarrass them, leading to hostility to English. But if you can turn those sentences into a chant, then you can get that student engaged in class. Are they reading in that moment and improving that skill? No. I completely concede that. But if you can make the class fun and interesting then hopefully you can get them to think about what they can do to get better and improve so that they can take part in other activities of class as well.

I think that I do my best to be as open and flexible in class. When students walk into my classroom it is usually the first time I have seen them in six months or so. I have to take a moment in the beginning to figure out every student's level. Always start with a smile and after a few quick questions and maybe a joke or funny picture we are on our way.

I will try to be more open and accessible for students. Usually after lunch teachers can be found in the staffroom having a coffee, but why not take a walk around the school and chat with students on their break and out of the classroom. I have the time available and they can't be hurt by a few moments of English language interaction, even though I know it terrifies some students. Hopefully this will relax them in other settings.

My Theory

A lot of how I feel about planning just comes down to the nature of where I work. English centers by nature see a wide swath of students with an even wider range of English abilities. I think in this situation you must be flexible in planning and preparation. If I start a class and the students can all speak and answer my intro questions then I am going to do my theme-room role play very differently than if they cannot name 'airplane' in English. If I had the same students every week and had a chance to teach them once or twice a week I would love to create intricate lessons with tasks to be completed. In the situation I am in now I think a hard and fast way would not be conducive for the large, varied selection of students that I see.

I think that I am very flexible, as I said each class is evaluated in the first minute. Just watching their reaction to questions and seeing if they can respond. Classes at a higher level have students taking a larger role. Classes that remain silent or struggle to respond are given slightly less to do. I feel like this hooks back into my principles but I really think it is important to note and I'm not afraid to say in this sort of situation I think it is effective and I will continue to plan extensively and at the same time loosely.

My Practice

I am surprised by the sheer volume of questions I ask in a lesson. I know I'm a teacher but four questions a minute seems like a lot. On the other hand in cooking class for 3rd grade I asked under two questions a minute. It feels like a very wide spread. I am interested in how many questions is an appropriate level for students of that age. I also find it shocking how often I allowed less than a second to pass before something was said in the 3rd grade Airplane lesson. It is so many times above the other classes that it makes me reconsider what sort of lesson I had. Was it just in my head that students did not understand me? It has the second most questions but dwarfs the 4th grade Airplane lesson which has more questions.

I also did not realize how I really lean on 'okay.' I think it is probably something that I do more with younger students and I can see that happening more, especially after I actually listened to the pizza lesson. I think that it is a good idea to not use that as much, I should be able to use other means for confirmation of understanding with students. Something like TPR (total physical response) or 'Simon says' with actions that are involved in the class. This will hopefully help students' comprehension and be a fun activity.

These are the most concrete things I have here. I know that I can change these and I look forward to making myself better with this information. I will absolutely try to manage my questions and the time I leave before speaking again better. I don't want to inhibit students by overloading them with language and I need to be more aware of that in the heat of the moment in class.

My Critical Reflections Beyond Practice

I have lived this situation for over a year now so it does not come as a mighty surprise to me. I guess that thing that really connects here is that night classes come at a cost of time to relax and that wears us down over time. Hopefully this can be changed through mediation.

Reflective Break

- What is your overall appraisal of Richard's reflections above?
- What is your understanding of the three different themes of approach-ability, art-oriented conceptions, and curiosity that seemed to emerge from Richard's journey?

Conclusion

This chapter has moved the discussion from the previous chapters on principles and tools of RP to actual practices where teachers focus on different aspects of reflection. The chapter explored the reflections of one experienced teacher in regard to teaching EFL in South Korea, as expressed through his philosophy, principles, theory, practice, and critical reflections. The results revealed that the common themes of approachability, art-oriented conceptions, and curiosity emerged in all aspects of his reflections. However, these themes did not emerge in the same form in each aspect of Richard's reflections, but rather as uniquely influential parts of a larger whole. The holistic framework for teacher reflection employed in Richard's journey provided multiple filters through which these various parts could be viewed. Moreover, while bringing otherwise unseen features to light, the recursive nature of this type of reflection allowed each aspect to be viewed as simultaneously separate from, and interconnected with, all other aspects. The complex and dynamic nature of this type of reflection attests to the importance of frequent RP for gaining a complete understanding of the factors that influence what teachers do in the classroom. The analysis has focused on the reflections of only one teacher, and that can be limiting I realize; nevertheless, by examining one teacher's progress through a multi-dimensional process of reflection, this chapter can provide language teachers with information that may guide their own reflective journeys, in whichever way they choose.

Chapter 6
Cultivating Reflective Practice

Introduction

So far I have outlined and discussed various definitions, levels, typologies, principles, practices, and tools of reflective practice (RP). All make up the basic ingredients of RP (later in this chapter I call them the *product* of RP) but they do not guarantee that it will be implemented by individual teachers or within institutions. For individuals to implement reflection beyond the mere during, before, or after class they must have a particular disposition that enables them to consider reflecting systematically on their practice. The reason for this is that reflection in an organized manner takes time and effort, and with all the textbooks out there in English language teaching (ELT) with associated instructor guides telling them what to do, some teachers may wonder why they should bother to implement reflection: why not just follow the book (and instructor's manual) for each lesson and let it be. However these are the very teachers who are first to complain about boredom or the monotony of having to follow the textbook and why they feel burnout as a result. So this chapter will address the type of disposition that will help teachers to face their reflections of their practice to enable them to become empowered professionals who provide maximum opportunities for their students' learning.

Institutions also wonder why they should encourage their teachers to reflect or encourage a culture of reflection either by individual teachers or in groups of teachers, or indeed, encourage teacher evaluation through RP. Some administrators may suggest that teachers, if they are qualified and trained, should know what to do in the classroom each day so they wonder why teachers need this type of professional development and how it can help the institution. Cultivating a climate of reflection within the institution has several benefits – most importantly better student learning (which is the reason for most institutions to exist after all!) because confident teachers can better communicate their teaching methods so that they provide an overall positive class atmosphere where optimum opportunities are provided for their students to learn. For that to happen, though, institutions must take specific steps to ensure that such a reflective approach to teaching and learning occurs by carefully cultivating different measures that ensure such a positive institutional collaborative environment. Yes, individual teachers have been 'told' to reflect either in teacher education programs or within institutions; however, this has basically been a mandatory ritual for most teachers where they are judged from predetermined criteria about what to reflect on and as such not much teacher development takes place.

This chapter outlines and discusses how RP can be cultivated individually and within an institution. Cultivating RP within an institution enables a more meaningful developmental and collaborative process for its teachers and administrators. RP will be more powerful if it is more collegial and if everyone sees its benefits as an integral part of organizational life in such educational settings. However, before we can encourage a culture of reflection in the school, we must first cultivate a reflective disposition in individual teachers within the school.

Cultivating a Reflective Disposition: From Product to Process

So far in this book I have discussed RP largely in terms of its product. However, in this chapter I focus more on a neglected aspect: the *process* of RP in language education, i.e., what *process* best helps teachers practice reflection? A process includes a systematic way of thinking that includes having a disposition to reflect that ends with meaning-making. However, what is missing in many of the discussions on RP in many fields of study is the need for teachers to develop such a reflective disposition so that they can engage in reflection in a meaningful manner. As Dewey's (1933) work on reflective thinking has suggested there can be no true reflection without a teacher developing a set of attitudes that he or she must consider before engaging in RP. Dewey noted that these dispositions are not passive attitudes, but a desire to actively consider multiple viewpoints of all people concerned. These attitudes I believe (after over 35 years working with this concept) are at the heart of the reflective process and the lack of them makes 'reflection' a ritual rather than a worthwhile developmental experience. It is not enough to develop knowledge of reflective methods and strategies (or the products), but also develop necessary character attitudes to accompany the reflective process, which include open-mindedness, responsibility, and whole-heartedness. I will discuss these three attitudes as they apply to TESOL and to my own teaching.

Unfortunately, though, and just like our continual methods fetish in language teaching, many scholars and practitioners over the years seem to have focused solely on the strategies and methods associated with achieving some fast and neat end product of reflection. This has resulted in turning reflection into a mechanical act that practices what Dewey warned against, reflection as routine action. Dewey (1933) ironically considered that such routine action can lead to achieving a pre-desired end while the means for getting those ends remains problematic. Above all, Dewey (1933: 17) considered reflection a form of freedom from routine behavior:

> Reflection emancipates us from merely impulsive and merely routine activity, it enables us to direct our activities with foresight and to plan according to ends-in-view or purposes of which we are aware, to act in deliberate and intentional fashion, to know what we are about when we act.

Reflective action, as Dewey (1933: 9) suggests, entails 'active, persistent, and careful consideration of any belief or supposed form of knowledge in the light of the grounds that support it and the further conclusions to which it leads.' Thus, reflection is not a point of view with end products (however well-intentioned), but a process of planned exploration and examination of the means (process and context) associated with reflection. The means associated with reflection must also be accompanied by a disposition to reflect, or a willingness to actively challenge the comfortable and (for many) taken for granted parts of our professional lives and undergo the trouble of searching while at the same time enduring a state of suspense as we do not know what we will find. As Dewey (1910: 13) noted, 'Reflective thinking is always more or less troublesome because it involves overcoming the inertia that inclines one to accept suggestions at their face value; it involves willingness to endure a condition of mental unrest and disturbance.' Dewey goes on to maintain that the essence of reflective thinking is the suspension of judgment and that this 'suspense is likely to be somewhat painful' but that the:

> most important factor in the training of good mental habits consists in acquiring the attitude of suspended conclusion, and in mastering the various methods of searching for new materials to corroborate or to refute the first suggestions that occur. To maintain the state of doubt and to carry on systematic and protracted inquiry – these are the essentials of thinking.

Thus, reflection entails that the practitioner not only has knowledge of the methods and strategies of reflective practice, but also cultivates a reflective 'disposition' to be able to carry out the process of reflection. In other words, attitude matters if one wants to engage in reflective inquiry in meaningful ways. Dewey (1933: 30) has maintained that knowledge of the strategies and methods of RP are not enough because 'there must be the desire, the will, to employ them. This is an affair of personal disposition.'

However, the term 'disposition' can mean different things to different people. For example, some may think it a particular habit or an attitude, an outlook or a particular temperament, or even in terms of a person's personality. It most likely includes all of these.

Dewey (1933: 28) suggests:

> No matter how much an individual knows as a matter of hearsay and information, if he [sic] has not attitudes and habits of this sort, he is not intellectually educated. He lacks the rudiments of mental discipline. And since these habits are not a gift of nature (no matter how strong the aptitude for acquiring them); since, moreover, the casual circumstances of the natural and social environment are not enough to compel their acquisition, the main office of education is to supply conditions that make for their cultivation. The formation of these habits is the training of mind.

Further, he states (1933: 30): 'there must be understanding of the forms and techniques that are the channels through which these attitudes operate to best advantage.'

So how does one cultivate such a reflective disposition? Dewey (1933) pointed out that there is a duality attached to reflection; yes, it is cognitive in every sense of the word, but a reflective disposition must also be accompanied by a set of three essential attitudes that must be cultivated to engage in reflective inquiry: *open-mindedness*, *wholeheartedness*, and *responsibility*. Dewey (1933: 139) has noted that all three of these attitudes are not only important in 'order that the habit of thinking in a reflective way may be developed ... they are traits of personal character that have to cultivated.'

I will discuss these three essential attitudes in some detail in terms of their implications for language education using examples from my own teaching career. However, for now I operationalize *open-mindedness* as a desire to listen to more than one side of an issue so that we can give attention to possible alternative views; *responsibility* as careful consideration of the consequences to which an action leads – in other words, what the impact of our reflection is, as well as who is impacted by our reflection; and *wholeheartedness* as the ability to overcome fears and uncertainties so that we may continuously review our practice. For Dewey, practitioners should develop these attitudes or qualities in order to create space for reflection and as teachers take responsibility for their decisions and actions.

Open-mindedness

Dewey (1933: 136) defined the disposition or attitude of open-mindedness as 'freedom from prejudice, partisanship, and such other habits as close the mind and make it unwilling to consider new problems and entertain new ideas.' However, he noted that open-mindedness is not the same as empty-mindedness, which he likens to hanging out a sign saying 'Come right in; there is no one at home,' which is not the equivalent of hospitality (Dewey, 1933: 183). Rather, he continued, there is a 'willingness to let experiences accumulate and sink in and ripen, which is an essential of development.' Thus, as we have noted in an earlier chapter, Dewey (1933: 136) maintains that to be truly open-minded one must have: 'an active desire to listen to more sides than one; to give heed to facts from whatever source they come; to give full attention to alternative possibilities; to recognize the possibility of error even in the beliefs that are dearest to us.'

Open-mindedness suggests that we need to 'let go' of being right all the time and that we should question our thinking and doubts in a kind of self-observation in order to gain more insight into our actions, thoughts, and learning. As Dewey (1933) noted, the alteration of old beliefs may require difficult work. We need to re-examine our beliefs and practices and may discover that what we do needs to be changed – in other words, we may need to 'admit that a belief to which we have once committed ourselves is wrong' (Dewey, 1933: 136).

So how does all this impact language teaching and how do teachers remain open-minded and question their philosophy, assumptions, and beliefs? How can we in language education implement this first attitude that Dewey so passionately argued is essential for reflective inquiry to be meaningful? This may sound easier than it seems, because most people will consider that they are open-minded. I have given talks and workshops all over the world over the past few years, and when I ask teachers if they are open-minded enough to consider that their current beliefs may be incorrect and need some readjustment, most suggest that they are very open-minded and are eager to examine and re-evaluate their beliefs. However, when I begin to discuss the details of intensive reflections about teacher beliefs and practices, many teachers become a bit uncomfortable and some are resistant to change. One of the questions I ask in such workshops concerning the idea of remaining open-minded is: *Do I consider why I teach my lesson(s) in a particular way, or am I faking it?*

This question can be somewhat of a shock for some teachers because the idea of 'faking' teaching is rather insulting to many. Yet, this was my own beginning as an English as a second language (ESL) teacher in Korea when in 1983, after five years of teaching the same way (group discussions in most classes regardless of the students' level), I began to wonder what was really happening in my lessons. My classes and lessons seemed to be going 'well,' and the students seemed happy with them. However, I often felt some unease but could not say exactly why until one day I began to ask questions about my teaching and to wonder what was *really* happening in my English lessons. In fact, I still remember the particular class I was teaching when I allowed myself to ask whether the students were really learning or just practicing their mistakes. I wondered if the lesson was successful, why was it successful, and many more such questions. I realized, somewhat painfully, that I would have to remain open-minded about my approach to my teaching from this day on, because I felt like I had been somewhat faking it up to that point.

The word 'faking' seems very strong, but I now consider that I think I was not as genuine a teacher as I should have been because I was not fully aware what was really happening in my lessons; in fact I was too scared to examine my teaching. I have continued to ask myself that question because I consider it important, and also because it serves as a continual reminder that I should always be alert to what is *really* happening in my classes. I also continued to ask this question in my work-shops and recently one teacher admitted that she too has felt uneasy about her lessons for the past ten years as an ESL teacher. She felt that she did not know what her students were learning, and wrote me the following short note after taking one of my workshops: 'Before I always felt like there was something missing and I almost felt like I was faking it. And now, I know after reflection that there still are things to be learned, but I know that I won't be faking it anymore.'

While I maintain that the particular lesson in 1983 at a university in Seoul, Korea was the first time I consciously reflected on my practice, I was in fact introduced to the concept a lot earlier – in my first year of teaching, in Ireland. I just did not know it then; I was to realize it when I began studying the concept of RP. It relates to another difficult question I ask teachers to reflect on in my workshops related to the attitude or disposition of open-mindedness: *Do I actively seek student input into how and what I teach?* The following is my personal story that outlines a very early critical incident in my professional teaching life which led me to reflect on my level of open-mindedness in terms of the importance of listening to my students and my need to admit that I could be wrong sometimes.

As a student-teacher on a teaching practice assignment in a high school in Dublin in 1977, I taught a class in business English to junior high school students. One morning during class, in my fourth week or so, a student suddenly shouted out: 'Teacher you are stupid!' I was astonished, as I had no idea at that moment how to respond. Although I was in shock for a few moments, I remember that I said to the boy that he could and should not say this to me, his teacher or any teacher, and that he should write a letter of apology to me before I would let him back to my class. I then asked him to leave for the remainder of that lesson. Just before class on the following day he handed me a letter which he said was a written apology. In that letter (which I still have today) he wrote: 'Teacher, I called you stupid because you were stupid because you gave us the same homework the day before and that is why you are stupid.'

When I read that note, I realized that he was correct as I had mistakenly given the class the same homework on two successive days. I also realized that even though we may think that students may not be listening to their teachers, in fact, they are. Unfortunately, the student who made the statement was actually deemed a 'problem' student by his regular teachers, in that he was always at the center of any class activity that the teachers had difficulty controlling; however, I had always had a good relationship with him probably because he reminded me of when I was a student at his age. I have never forgotten this 'critical incident' and now after many years working within the topic of RP, I realize it was my first introduction to Schön's (1983) reflection-in-action (my immediate response to the student's statement) and reflecting-on-action (my later responses). Over the years, I have had many more occasions where I have experienced both reflection-in-action moments and reflection-on-action examples in different classrooms, contexts, and countries. However, it was that early classroom example that has stayed with me over the years, although I had no real understanding of its true meaning until I began to read Schön's (1983) seminal work on reflective practice (see below for more on this).

Reflective Break

- How open-minded should a teacher be?
- Are you open-minded?
- If yes, how do you know?
- Can you give an account of an example of how you are open-minded as a teacher?

Responsibility

Dewey said that responsibility in the context of fostering reflection means considering the consequences of what one has done (or actions) and what one has learned, and that one must have the attitude of responsibility to complete any project. For him (1933: 138) a responsible attitude is one where people 'consider the consequences of a projected step; it means to be willing to adopt these consequences when they follow reasonably from any position already taken.' However, he says that it is not uncommon to see people continue to hold on to false beliefs: 'They profess certain beliefs but are unwilling to commit themselves to the consequences that flow from them. The result is mental confusion.'

If we look closely at responsibility as a means of fostering reflection, we can see that this attitude concerns considering the effect of our reflections on ourselves, our students, the community in which we teach, and the greater society of which we are members. So the main question I ask at my workshops related to the attitude of responsibility is: *What is the impact of what you do and your reflections on what you do at the descriptive, conceptual, and critical levels?* This question coincides with Christopher Day's (1993) notion of teachers acting within three different hierarchical levels of reflection (see chapter 1): the first is where teachers focus their reflections on behavioral actions (*descriptive reflection*), the second where teachers also include justifications of these reflections based on current theories of teaching (*conceptual reflection*), while at the third level teachers include the first two and look beyond theories and practices to examine their ethical, moral, and social ramifications (*critical reflection*).

Descriptive reflection is where teachers reflect at the level of classroom actions, and this means systematically collecting data about what they actually do rather than suggesting what they think they do, because what teachers say they do in their lessons can be a lot different from what they actually do. This evidence-based approach to reflection encourages teachers to avoid making instructional decisions based on impulse or routine; rather, they are encouraged to use the data they have obtained so that they can make more informed decisions about their practice. Richards & Lockhard's (1994: 1) definition summarizes this evidence-based reflective approach as they encourage teachers to 'collect data about their teaching, examine their attitudes, beliefs, assumptions, and teaching practices, and use the information obtained as a basis for critical reflection about teaching.' In my workshops I ask questions related to helping teachers reflect at the descriptive level, such as: *What do you do in your lessons? How do you do it?*

The level of *conceptual reflection* encourages teachers to consider the different reasons they do what they do. At this level of reflection, teachers conceptualize their practice and ideally they can compare what they do to what their immediate colleagues do. These conceptualizations can also be compared to what they read about in a literature review of particular topics of interest. In my workshops questions related to helping teachers reflect at the conceptual level of reflection include: *Why do you do it? What is the result?*

Critical reflection, as Brookfield (1995: 8) has noted, has two purposes: '(1) To understand how considerations of power undergird, frame and distort educational processes and interactions. (2) To question assumptions and practices that seem to make our teaching lives easier but actually work against our own best long term interests.' Although largely ignored within TESOL until very recently, scholars such as Graham Crooks have called for a more critical second language pedagogy that includes 'teaching for social justice, in ways that support the development of active, engaged citizens who ... will be prepared to seek out solutions to the problems they define and encounter, and take action accordingly' (Crooks, 2013: 8). Questions related to helping teachers reflect at the critical level in my workshops are: *What is the impact of what you do at the political, moral, and ethical levels? Whose interests are being served by your teaching and the school you teach in?*

Reflective Break

- Are you responsible?
- If yes, how do you know?
- Can you give an account of an example of how you are responsible as a teacher?

Wholeheartedness

When a reflective practitioner has a *wholehearted* attitude, he or she takes up a project with a *total commitment* to reflection, and as such, 'throws himself into it' (Dewey, 1933: 137) with an open heart, care and mindfulness. Dewey (1933) goes on to say that 'There is no greater enemy of effective thinking than divided interest ... [but] when a person is absorbed, the subject carries him on.' Thus a teacher who is excited to look at his or her practice does so with undivided attentions and 'questions occur to him spontaneously; a flood of suggestions pour in on him; further inquiries and readings are indicated and followed' (Dewey, 1933: 137). In other words, a reflective teacher who has a wholehearted attitude will reflect-*in*-action, -*on*-action and -*for*-action throughout his or her career. As Stanley (1998: 585) has noted, practioners reflect on all three levels 'when they look at their work in the moment (reflect-in-action) or in retrospect (reflect-on-action) in order to examine the reasons and beliefs underlying their actions and generate alternative actions for the future [reflect-for-action].'

Reflective Break

- Are you wholehearted?
- If yes, how do you know?
- Can you give an account of an example of how you are wholehearted as a teacher?
- Do you think that teachers should commit to reflection and take socially responsible decisions and actions? If yes, how?

Developing a School Culture of Reflection

In the previous section I outlined three essential attitudes that must be cultivated within the individual teacher who wishes to engage in reflective inquiry: *open-mindedness, wholeheartedness*, and *responsibility*. Of course, these three attitudes could equally be associated with the school or institution in which the individual teacher is practicing and reflecting. However, when considering the institution, we must realize that every institution has its own unique culture that must also be taken into consideration when trying to develop a philosophy of reflection throughout that institution.

Each school has its own culture that is noticeable to every new teacher and student although much of this may not be documented or even talked about. For example, a school has its own unique set of rituals that reflect its values and also shape the behavior and relationships of the people who work and study in that school. In more general terms, schools can have cultures that exist on a continuum from highly individualistic to collaborative where all the teachers are willing to help one another.

Schools or institutions that have a culture of individualism can be seen as places where colleagues have relationships characterized by non-committal type of existence – or as Lortie (1975: 195) puts it: 'live and let live, and help [only] when asked.' In this type of school culture, teachers 'have peers but no colleagues' (Feiman-Nemser & Floden, 1986: 508). Such a culture of individualism can damage the long-term interests of a school because nobody takes pride in their work as they remain on individual paths that can pull away from the center.

At the other end of the continuum, in schools or institutions that pursue a culture of collaboration, colleagues can be considered of major importance for the development of each other and are often referred as 'guides and guardians' (Zeichner, 1983: 9) rather than individualists. Such collaborations result in shared values and beliefs about teaching and learning and the sense that they are all there together working for their students' collective success.

However, I suspect that is a more realistic picture of school culture is one where several different 'teacher cultures' exist in one school and that teachers are usually faced with the dilemma of which one to adopt. It is also a fact, to which many experienced teachers will attest, that the existing culture of the school (whatever it may be) dictates the energy of that school very strongly, be it negative or positive. So it is important that, when encouraging teachers to engage in RP, the school's culture should be in keeping with this encouragement or it will not take on a school-wide ownership. It is up to the administration and school heads to build a culture of reflection out of the competing cultures that may exist in the school.

Schools and institutions can do a lot to develop a culture of reflection in the workplace. They can establish a system of teacher evaluation through self-reflection; they can engage in mentoring to guide less experienced teachers, or encourage team teaching for teachers to reflect with each other, as well as peer coaching and critical friendships for teachers to help each other; and they can also sponsor various events – within the school and outside in the community – that can foster a culture of reflection that establishes an overall vibrant and healthy working environment.

Reflective Break

- Should schools develop a culture of reflection?
- How can schools develop a culture of reflection?
- What type of culture exists in your school?
- Who decides what type of culture exists in a school?
- What roles should administrators and teachers play in developing a school culture?

Teacher Evaluation through Reflection

Reflection and assessment are deeply connected: the ability to reflect effectively requires that teachers self-assess, and the ability to self-assess also depends on the ability to reflect effectively. It is a fact of life for most TESOL teachers that they will be evaluated in some capacity several times in the course of their careers. Although each teacher evaluation may vary, the evaluation process invariably involves observations of some kind, of the teacher in action in the classroom, by someone who 'visits' or drops-in on one or more days to appraise 'features' of the teacher's teaching – usually the teachers' behavior in class. These 'features' are often pre-determined by others (inside or outside the school) and presented as checkmarks on what is commonly called a teacher evaluation form. Such approaches to teacher evaluation have many shortcomings that include the following: lack of agreement on what 'good' teaching is, ambiguity in the rating of teaching behavior, the top-down nature of the process.

Reflective Break

- How are you evaluated as a teacher in your school?

Teacher evaluations can be more collaborative, however, if both sides share the burden of evaluation, i.e., if teachers are given more responsibility in the evaluation process. In other words, we can *shift* the burden of evaluation from solely the shoulders of administrators and supervisors to a more sharing process where each teacher is required to compile a teaching portfolio that includes their philosophy, principles, theory, practice, and beyond practice reflections for the purposes of self-assessment as well as evaluation. Thus, if we consider teacher evaluation through RP this produces a more collaborative school environment and is beneficial to both the teacher who is being evaluated and the supervisor doing the evaluation (and the school) because in this process a teacher's development over time can be objectively discussed.

When teachers and supervisors approach teaching evaluation from a collaborative perspective, all sides enter a win-win situation because they all benefit from such a reflective approach. As the opening chapters of this book attest to, RP encourages teachers to take responsibility for making decisions in their practice and a reflective approach to teacher evaluation also encourages ownership of the teacher's self-assessment through reflecting on practice. When teachers and their supervisors collaborate with evaluations of the teachers' journey through the RP framework, it promotes and enhances their discussions because both are engaged in the reflective process.

Teachers can compile *teaching portfolios* as a means of shared evaluation. A teaching portfolio is a collection of information about a teacher's practice. It tells the story of the teacher's efforts, skills, abilities, achievements, and contributions to students, colleagues, institutions, academic disciplines, and the community. A teaching portfolio might include (but is not limited to) lesson plans, anecdotal records, student projects, class newsletters, videotapes, annual evaluations, and letters of recommendation. Overall it should reflect the teacher's philosophy, principles, theory, practice examples, and critical reflection. It should be remembered that the teaching portfolio is not a one-time snapshot of where the teacher is at present; it is a growing collection of carefully selected and recorded professional experiences, thoughts, and goals. After collecting and assembling all the materials for their teaching portfolios, teachers reflect with their supervisors on what they have put together and assess their current and future teaching plans. In such a manner teaching portfolios can provide teachers with opportunities for self-reflection and collaboration with colleagues in addition to opportunities to collaborate with the school for the purposes of teacher evaluation as well as plan individual professional development paths.

This idea of portfolios can be extended to student learning and assessment of that learning. Portfolios compiled by students can equally serve as means of assessment. Students need no longer memorize information for tests only to forget it immediately after; rather, they can explore and reflect on their own learning through their portfolios just as their teachers use teaching portfolios to reflect on their learning and teaching. Such self-assessment on both sides of the desk can go a long way towards building a culture of collaboration in a school where everyone is out to help, rather than hurt, each other.

Reflective Break

- Have you ever compiled a teaching portfolio? If yes, please explain what kind of portfolio you compiled and your reasons for compiling it.
- Possible contents of a teaching portfolio include the following items: lesson plans, student projects, class newsletters, videotapes, annual evaluations, and letters of recommendation. Can you think of any other items that you could include in your portfolio that tell the story of your efforts and skills as a teacher? List them.
- How long would it take you to compile the components of a teaching portfolio?
- Write out a professional development plan that includes how you will continue to reflect on your teaching.
- Update your current resume for this section of the teaching portfolio.

Mentoring

Another important collaborative relationship that can develop among teaching peers as well as the administration in a school is mentoring of some sort to help each other grow. A mentor is usually an experienced teacher who is appointed, or volunteers, to support a new teacher. These mentor teachers have usually been drawn from veteran teachers within a school who help beginners learn the philosophy, cultural values, and established sets of behaviors expected by the school employing them. Research indicates that beginner teachers who are mentored are more effective teachers in their early years, since they learn from guided practice rather than depending upon trial-and-error efforts alone. It was found that generally mentored novice teachers tend to leave the teaching profession at a rate lower than non-mentored novices.

Within English language teaching, Malderez & Bodoczky (1999: 4) describe five different roles that mentors can play 'to a greater or lesser degree': (1) They can be models who inspire and demonstrate. (2) They can be acculturators who show mentees the ropes. (3) They can be sponsors who introduce the mentees to the 'right people.' (4) They can be supporters who are there to act as sounding boards, should mentees need to let off steam. (5) They can be educators who act as sounding boards for the articulation of ideas to help new teachers achieve professional learning objectives.

Furthermore, an additional support system should be established within schools: the formal mentorship program should be complemented by a buddy system to help familiarize new teachers with the school routines. A buddy can be a critical friend who can coach and guide the new teacher while acting as a protector, shielding his/her protégé from potentially damaging situations and easing the new teacher into the culture of the school. For example, a buddy could be a less senior teacher who has developed some degree of expertise in reflective activities such as journal writing, action research, or video recording of lessons, and who can give practical advice to colleagues wishing to undertake these activities for the first time. This buddy could act as a mentor (but in a nonjudgmental manner) while observing the new teacher teach. Obtaining feedback without worrying about any negative implications would also go a long way in helping teachers to grow. However, if a buddy is going to help a new teacher through his/her first year, he/she should be encouraged to volunteer for the role. As a volunteer, the buddy should be a willing participant in the new teacher's induction and be given recognition for this important role by the school and the principal. This recognition could be in the form of a reduced teaching load for the buddy during the first semester of the beginner teacher's tenure.

Reflective Break

- Have you ever experienced mentoring?
- Was the mentor 'qualified'?
- Did the mentor inspire you?
- Did the mentor show you the ropes?
- Did the mentor introduce you to the 'right people'? If yes, who?
- Did you use the mentor as a sounding board?
- Did you use the mentor to let off steam?

Team Teaching

Team teaching is a type of critical friendship arrangement whereby two or more teachers cooperate as equals as they take responsibility for planning, teaching, and evaluating a class, a series of classes, or a whole course (Richards & Farrell, 2005). Team teaching involves collaborative partnership and it is important that, in order to develop the culture of reflection within the institution, teams gather voluntarily rather than this being imposed from above. Typically in such a collaboration teachers share accountability and responsibility for planning a class and or course, then teaching the class/course, completing follow-up work (i.e., evaluations/assessments), and making various decisions and outcomes.

Teachers usually cooperate as equals, though some elements of coaching may occur as they can define the roles and responsibilities that are most suitable for their own individual needs and situations. Richards & Farrell (2005) outline some of the following team teaching arrangements that teams can choose from, depending on what best meets their needs:

Equal partners: both teachers see themselves as having an equal experience and knowledge and so all decisions are shared equally for all stages of the lesson: planning, delivery, monitoring, and checking.

Leader and participant: one teacher is given or assumes a leadership role because he or she has more experience with team teaching.

Mentor and apprentice: one teacher is recognized as an expert teacher (and thus takes more responsibility) while the other is a novice.

Native/Advanced speaker and less proficient speaker: in some situations (such as in Japan's JET program) a native English language speaker or an advanced speaker of English may team teach with a less proficient speaker. In some cases the native/advanced speaker takes responsibility for those aspects of the lesson that are more

linguistically demanding, but in many cases the lesson takes place in the less proficient speaker's class so he or she must take responsibility for setting up the lesson.

Team teaching can promote collegiality, alleviates teachers' feeling of isolation,
and lowers student-teacher ratios in classrooms. It can build confidence in teachers
because the feedback is informal but free from bias; thus in addition it promotes
mutual trust and understanding between teachers in institutions. Team teaching
also enhances teaching techniques as teachers try out different activities in a supportive environment. Most of all, these collaborations promote reflection for both
teachers and students.

Reflective Break

- Have you ever experienced a team teaching relationship? If yes, describe
  your experiences.
- How was the relationship set up, and what different roles were played by
  each team member?
- Do you think it is possible for two teachers to take equal responsibility for
  planning and teaching a class? If not, why not?
- How can the students benefit from having two teachers teach the same
  lesson?
- Both teachers in a team teaching relationship have certain roles to play.
  Discuss these different roles and outline possible problems that may
  arise within each role.

Peer Coaching

Peer coaching is another collaborative arrangement between teachers in institutions that can promote a culture of reflection. It is different from team teaching
as it is intended to improve specific instructional techniques of one of the peers,
usually the observed teacher, in a supportive environment. It is non-evaluative as
the observer peer (usually a more experienced teacher in the institution) provides
constructive feedback in a safe learning environment so that the observed teacher
(less experienced) can develop new knowledge and skills and a deeper awarness of
his or her own teaching. Thus the more experienced teacher can take on a mentoring role (see above) even while both teachers view themselves as peers and equals.

There are different types of peer coaching arrangements such as technical coaching: a teacher may seek the assistance of another teacher who is experienced and
more knowledgeable in order to learn new teaching methods/techniques; collegial

coaching where two teacher-peers focus on refining their existing teaching practices; and challenge coaching where a problem arises and two teachers work jointly to resolve the problem (Richards & Farrell, 2005).

Peer coaching arrangements promote greater awareness and self-confidence as well as better collaboration among teachers in institutions. Peer coaching also improves the school climate because it facilitates the exchange of teaching methods, materials, approaches, and techniques. It also promotes the implementation of new strategies in the classroom and thus improves instructional skills (Richards & Farrell, 2005). Related to teacher evaluation through RP outlined in a previous section of this chapter, peer coaching provides an ongoing assessment of specific skills and teaching strategies which helps teachers to continuously reflect on their practice.

Reflective Break

- How can peer coaching benefit the teacher, the coach, and the school?
- Richards & Farrell (2005) suggest that feedback in a peer coaching relationship should take the form of 'No Praise, No Blame.' What is your understanding of this?
- The coach has a specific role to play in a peer coaching relationship. Discuss this role and outline possible problems that may arise between the teacher and the coach.

Critical Friends

Critical friends collaborate in a two-way mode that encourages discussion and reflection in order to improve the quality of language teaching and learning. A critical friendship in teaching entails entering into a collaborative arrangement with another teacher 'in a way which encourages talking with, questioning, and even confronting, the trusted other, in order to examine planning for teaching, implementation, and its evaluation' (Hatton & Smith, 1995: 41). This arrangement can lead to development of a culture of reflection in an institution if such friendships are encouraged by the administration; however, the friendships should be voluntary. In such arrangements, peers collaborate with trusted colleagues who give advice as a friends rather than consultants in a structured environment.

The composition of a critical friends group is ultimately decided by its members and a group can consist of from two to twelve members. Critical friends can stimulate self-reflection and encourage discussion to improve teaching and learning in a safe environment that leads to an increase in collegiality in the institution. The purpose of entering into critical friendships is for mutual development of the teachers as there is no hierarchy of expertise among the friends. As a result of entering into such arrangements, teachers can gain new and deeper understandings and insights about their practice and try out new ideas and strategies as they reflect on their practice. Critical friendships can help to highlight any gaps between beliefs and practices because, as Lakshmi (2014: 202) notes, 'Teachers constructed their own explanations of teaching derived from their own practices, and the explanations (or knowledge) were socially negotiated and restructured within their classrooms.' Indeed, Lakshmi (2014: 200) considers the collaboration involved in such arrangements as beneficial to their self-evaluation (see the earlier section): 'Teachers realized the need for collaborative work, and sought advice from their senior colleagues to solve their classroom problems and for their self-evaluation.'

Reflective Break

- Have you ever experienced a critical friendship relationship? If yes, describe your experience.
- What is your understanding of the term 'critical' in critical friendship relationships?
- When teachers meet as critical friends, they should focus more on the friend and less on the critical. Discuss this approach to critical friendship.

School Sponsored Events

School leaders and administrators can promote reflective practice as a school culture not only by encouraging teachers to examine and reflect on their practices collectively through teaching portfolios, critical friendships, and mentoring, but also by sponsoring specific reflective events. The institution as a result can begin to function as a community of professionals rather than as individuals working in isolation from each other. Developing school sponsored events creates a culture by building cohesive and professional relationships between teachers, administrators, and the wider community.

Such events can include brown-bag lunches where teachers share their knowledge with each other. Teachers can also bring in materials they use for teaching the various skills (e.g., speaking, listening, writing, and reading) and discuss them in such brown-bag meetings. This can lead to the development of materials as a collaborative effort that further connects teachers and administrators. The group can invite outside speakers who are experienced in a particular topic that interests the group. The school administration can encourage such events by allowing time off for teachers to prepare, as well as providing the space and refreshments.

The administrators can also support their teachers' attending different seminars and conferences outside the school. These teachers can share what they have learnt with the other teachers in brown-bag events or other such collaborative gatherings. Schools can also promote reading and discussion by building a professional library and encouraging reflection in teacher study groups on particular topics of interest. They can also arrange visits to other schools, where appropriate, to find out how reflective and professional development activities are conducted and supported there. By organizing and supporting various events, the school as a whole benefits and will attract more students as well as providing better opportunities to learn.

Reflective Break

- What events does your school sponsor?
- What events would you like your school to sponsor?

Conclusion

This chapter has discussed ways of developing a culture of refection in the individual and in the school or institution. The starting point for such a culture is the individual teacher who must first develop a reflective disposition or attitude. A reflective disposition entails teachers embracing three main character attitudes to accompany the reflective process: open-mindedness, responsibility, and whole-heartedness. Open-minded teachers realize that they may not be correct all the time and that they may need to change their attitudes to parts of their practice even if they have lots of experience. Responsible teachers note that their actions and words have a huge impact on their students, their colleagues, and their community. Wholehearted teachers realize that they will never really know the answers so they will continuously strive to reflect in, on, and for action.

As we have also seen above, encouraging and developing a culture of reflection within schools and institutions is of equal importance. This can be achieved by schools promoting self-assessment, mentoring, peer coaching, team teaching, and critical friendships (among other collaborative activities for teachers) to develop a positive school climate where everybody learns. Indeed, if the school takes the lead and sponsors various events that encourage such collaborations among teachers, everybody benefits. When teachers are encouraged to embrace reflection personally, professionally, and institutionally as a way of life, they will be better able to provide optimum learning opportunities for their students.

Chapter 7

Ten Questions for Reflection

Introduction

Since its resurgence in the 1980s reflective practice (RP) has mushroomed among the different professions as a mark of professional competence. This fascinating and complex topic has, as the contents of this book have suggested, generated many different approaches, models, and typologies that at times have resulted in a great deal of uncertainty over the meaning of reflection. Many of the approaches that have proliferated are based on different theoretical underpinnings and some are even used to rationalize existing practices in a rather unreflective manner. Additionally, many typologies are based mainly on the work of Dewey and/or Schön but I would also posit that these typologies may not fully understand what these two wonderful scholars were *really* saying about reflection.

As mentioned before, the current vagueness associated with reflection and RP poses serious problems for teacher educators, teachers, administrators, and teacher education and development programs. In addition, the ambiguity of the concept of RP has led some scholars in TESOL to question the whole value of encouraging teachers to engage in reflection, wondering if this engagement will improve teaching or lead to better teachers than those who do not engage in any systematic reflection. Some others have dismissed RP as just another bandwagon within a field (education and TESOL) which has witnessed many bandwagons over the years. These are all valid concerns, and so in this final chapter I will attempt to address as many of the ambiguities as possible by tackling the following ten questions related to reflective practice:

1. Has RP become just another bandwagon?
2. Has TESOL embraced RP?
3. How can we make RP workable for all teachers?
4. Is it possible to teach pre-service language teachers to reflect?
5. Can reflection be faked?

6. Is it possible to assess reflection?
7. Can RP be used for teacher evaluation?
8. What are some of the criticisms of RP?
9. What are the benefits of engaging in RP?
10. What is the future for RP?

Has Reflective Practice Become Just Another Bandwagon?

This first question is very important because it has been used by some scholars as a means of outright dismissal of the concept of RP both within TESOL and in general education studies. Some have talked about the appeal of the 'reflection bandwagon' in pre-service education though pre-service teachers do not know how to reflect, while others have suggested that experienced teachers do not want to reflect on their work because RP does not consider the realities of their work. Or, as Loughran (2002: 42) has noted: 'Reflection has developed a variety of meanings as the bandwagon has traveled through the world of practice.' So I will first analyze what a bandwagon is, and then examine if RP fits under this banner.

Bandwagons came to prominence in political discourse many years ago when people attempted to push products or ideas without having much behind them. According to Clarke (1982: 438) bandwagons come from 'within a political campaign – exaggerated campaign promises of hucksters who will give you the moon if you'll just give them your vote.' Bandwagons have many different features such as (from Clarke, 1982: 439):

- They are the latest word, the trendy, the fashionable, the most-up-to-date in methods, materials, techniques.
- They have a carnival appeal, in that 'bandwagoneers [are] mindless, [have] a total orientation to the here and now, and a willingness to regard people as objects to be used for external purposes.'
- They are extremist – they wipe out what has gone on before.
- They are authoritarian – (a) they insist on *only* one right way; (b) they rely on the words of the masters.
- They are all-encompassing – no truth remains unexplained.
- They are dramatic and appealing – they claim to solve all problems.
- They promote their own bag of tricks – success means adhering to their prescribed beliefs and techniques.

I would suggest that RP should not and does not claim to provide the latest word on teacher development: it is only one particular movement among many that teachers have the right to choose from. Although there are strategies (I will address this again later) attached to engaging in RP, I do not believe it is bound by 'the most-up-to-date in methods, materials, or techniques,' because it is a 'way of life' as I pointed out in one of the principles in chapter 3. RP is also not orientated to the here and now without considering the past and the future – as reflection-*on*-action and reflection-*for*-action along with reflecting-*in*-action attest to.

In addition, RP is not an extremist approach to professional development as it does not attempt in any way to wipe out what has gone on before it. In fact if one examines Dewey's (1933) reflective inquiry, one can see that it is the precursor to the current action research and teacher research movement in many TESOL circles, yet this is rarely, if ever, acknowledged by the later scholars. Also, RP is not authoritarian in any manner as it does not insist that there is only one right way to approach a teacher's professional development. Although there may seem to be overreliance on both Dewey's and Schön's (the masters?) work, I have attempted to point out that there are also other typologies that have taken hold that under-pin different theoretical orientations to these two great scholars. I will also point out later in this chapter the promising research that has taken hold in the field of TESOL which shows that RP as a concept is maturing, by noting how context and subject matter impact its implementation.

Finally, I would also suggest that RP is not an all-encompassing approach to teacher professional development and a lot remains unexplained, as this chapter notes. There are a lot of questions that need to be continued to be asked about this complex concept but the fact that we are asking them does not mean we should dismiss the concept. Many scholars, including myself, readily admit to the point that engaging in RP will not solve all teachers' problems; I believe it is not designed to do this as it is not a prescriptive approach to teacher development and it does not promote any particular 'bag of tricks.' What we have to be on guard against is the mandatory nature that RP has taken on in some institutions where admin-istrators are using it by getting teachers to adhere to *their* prescribed and pre-determined set of checklists that masquerade as reflection. The result of this approach is that many teachers fake their reflections to give the administrators what they are looking for.

I agree, as Clarke (1982: 444) noted, that a bandwagon gains momentum 'when slogans and bumper stickers begin to replace critical appraisal and cautious experimentation with ideas, when the masses begin to gather around the wagon and the carnival barker replaces the professional.' This aspect, the critical appraisal of the concept of RP for language teacher education and development, is very important; we as a profession must not blindly accept RP because 'it rings true for most people as something useful to practice' (Loughran, 2002: 33). We must be on guard against the flowery delivery of messages concerning the common sense of reflection and critically examine and appraise the content of reflection if it is to be useful for language teachers in their quest to provide optimum learning conditions for their students.

> **Reflective Break**
> - What is a bandwagon for you?
> - Has reflective practice become another educational bandwagon?
> - Go through each of the defining characteristics of bandwagons above and consider if the concept of reflective practice can be included in any of them.

Has TESOL Embraced Reflective Practice?

The term 'bandwagon' has also been used to describe RP with the field of TESOL, with some scholars (I will not name them) being very skeptical about the whole RP movement and especially the impact of engaging in RP for teachers. Some ask questions such as: will engaging in reflective practice improve the quality of teaching, will reflection result in better teacher performance, and the like. These are difficult (but important) questions to answer, because, when one says 'improved quality' or 'better performance' in teaching, then do we assume that we have an agreed baseline of what 'good quality' or 'good teacher performance' is in order to make judgments about any improvements to these? In this section I will outline and briefly discuss the findings of my own reflections on RP in TESOL (from Farrell, 2018a); as Akbari (2007: 205) noted: 'It is good to reflect, but reflection itself also requires reflection.'

I reviewed studies in academic journals on the practices that encourage TESOL teachers to reflect (I did not include books, monographs, chapters or the like) and I discovered a robust number of articles devoted to TESOL and reflection: 138. These were evenly divided between pre-service and in-service TESOL teachers, with only a few studies having both pre-service and in-service teachers as participants. That nearly 50% of all the studies reviewed focused on the practices that encouraged in-service/experienced TESOL teachers to reflect contradicts what some TESOL scholars have recently suggested about the paucity of RP research related to in-service/experienced teachers' reflections on their work. So right from the start, the answer is yes, TESOL has embraced the concept of RP because it leads to enhanced awareness of important issues for both pre-service and in-service TESOL teachers (Farrell, 2018a; also 2016b).

More specifically, Farrell (2018a) noted that when TESOL teachers were encouraged to reflect on their *philosophy* (mostly through accessing their personal histories) most studies reported that teachers could better understand their teacher identity origins, formation, and development. When TESOL teachers were encouraged to reflect on *principles* (mostly through metaphor analysis and reflective writing), most (but not all) studies reviewed reported that, as teachers became more aware of their previously tacitly held assumptions, values, and beliefs about teaching and learning, they were better able to re-evaluate them in light of their new knowledge. When teachers were encouraged to reflect on *theory* (mostly through lesson planning) the studies reported that pre-service TESOL teachers were able to build repertoires and knowledge of instruction while in-service TESOL teachers benefited most from accessing their theory through collective and collaborative lesson-planning conferences. When TESOL teachers were encouraged to reflect on their *practice*, the results indicated that some kind of feedback during pre- and post-observation conferences in groups of some form (e.g., with or without video recordings of the lessons) can facilitate such reflections especially for pre-service TESOL teachers. For in-service TESOL teachers the results indicated that although most teachers reported an overall positive impact of classroom observations because they lead to enhanced awareness of theory and practice connections, they also noted the potential adverse reactions to being observed by others, so the affective side of classroom observations should be considered. The results also reveal that other forms of post-observation feedback, similar as with pre-service teachers – such as the use of teacher groups, teacher study groups, or critical friends – may not only stimulate reflection on theory/practice connections but also alleviate some of the affective issues and misgivings about being observed. When TESOL teachers were encouraged to reflect *beyond practice* in combination with philosophy, principles, theory, and practice, most of the studies reported that the teachers reflected well beyond their classroom teaching practices on such issues as: the textbooks they are given to teach, the syllabus and curriculum they are given, and their working conditions – especially what they are expected to do by the administration as against what they think their professional roles are.

Because most of the studies revealed that many TESOL teachers tended to focus their reflections on their practice while ignoring the critical aspects of their work (see also chapter 1 where definitions within TESOL tended to also ignore the moral and critical aspects of reflection), Farrell (2018a) recommended that teacher educators and teacher education programs expand their TESOL teachers' reflections to include philosophy and go beyond practice by incorporating some kind of community-based service learning project (that integrates classroom instruction with community service activities) into TESOL teacher preparation courses.

The results of Farrell's (2018a) review revealed the global reach and the robust nature of the concept of RP research within the TESOL profession. The study concluded that TESOL has embraced the concept of RP but it must be careful to be on guard against others using it as a tool to 'fix' problems because this keeps TESOL teachers down, treating them as technicians and consumers of research rather than generators of their own research. Thus we must now consider how we can make RP workable for all TESOL teachers.

Reflective Break

- Should TESOL embrace reflective practice as a viable educational concept?
- Do you think TESOL as a field has or has not embraced reflective practice?
- Are you familiar with all the research (e.g., as outlined in Farrell, 2018a) that has been conducted in TESOL on the practices that encourage TESOL teachers to reflect?
- Have you conducted any research on reflective practice?

How Can We Make Reflective Practice Workable for All TESOL Teachers?

For sure, the reflective teaching model is a demanding one as it asks a lot of teachers, both pre-service and in-service teachers. Reflection can also be destructive if teachers continuously blame themselves for things not their fault, such as a lesson not going according to plan: perhaps the students were not in the mood to study and it had nothing to do with the teacher or his or her planning and delivery. In addition teachers complain that they have no space or time to reflect although they perform informal reflections all of the time on the way to school or on the way home. So the question of how we can make RP workable for all teachers is an important one.

For example, many scholars wonder if pre-service teachers can really engage in any meaningful reflection given that they already have heavy demands placed on them in their foundation and theoretical courses as well as the cognitive overload they experience in everyday lessons during the practicum or their first year teaching. I will attempt to answer these questions as I believe RP is a workable approach to a teacher's professional development, but we need to be realistic especially in what we ask the teachers to do.

I would consider the following three basic prerequisites a necessity to make RP workable:

- *Time*: All involved with the reflective process must consider how time is provided for. In my early model of RP (see Farrell, 2004) I suggested the need to provide for four different types of time: individual (time to commit to reflection), activity (time to spend on each activity of reflection), development (set time to develop), period of reflection (time frame as a whole to reflect) – see chapter 2 for more on this.
- *Opportunity for reflection*: There should be a provision of tasks/activities for teachers that involve reflection – such as group discussions, journal writing, classroom observations, and many more as outlined in this book. These can include the following:
  o Guided observation tasks (and written report)
  o Analysis of classroom data (e.g., lesson transcripts, lesson plans)
  o Written assignments
  o Journals
  o Dialogues with critical friends
  o Portfolios
  o Critical incident analysis
  o Case studies
  o Teacher beliefs inventories
  o Group discussion of readings
  o Problem-solving through brainstorming
  o Materials evaluation
- *Training*: Separate training is necessary to help build reflective skills. We cannot just 'tell' pre-service teachers to 'reflect' without training them to do so. Learning to teach is like learning to drive for the first time. Here we must concentrate consciously on every movement we make: change the gears from neutral to first by taking off my right foot from the brake and putting it gently on the accelerator while at the same time easing my left foot off the clutch; also watch and steer the car while I am doing this. Can you imagine how you would respond if someone asked you to reflect on this while you were doing it (reflection-*in*-action) or right after (reflection-*on*-action) it was completed for the first time? Just like learning to drive, novice teachers may have no spare processing capacity for thinking while they are teaching. After the event, I have also found that teachers have little

spare time to reflect because of the many demands placed on them by all the different courses they have to take. It is also difficult for novice teachers to detach themselves from the event that has just taken place. In the early stages of teaching novice teachers are too much involved with the events themselves, and it seems that they tend to recall events of the lesson less accurately than do more experienced teachers. Also, they may not have the schema for making judgments. Therefore, reflective skills must be taught separately from teaching practice, because there would be too much cognitive overload involved if it was all presented together. Other sub-skills of reflection that teachers would need training in is how to make beliefs explicit; how to formulate questions about teaching; how to collect and record evidence about teaching (observe, collect data from their own and other teachers' classrooms); how to understand the evidence obtained; how to explore alternatives; how to apply insights.

Reflective Break

- What prerequisites would you suggest are necessary for reflection to be workable?
- What are essential opportunities that should be provided for TESOL teachers to reflect?

Is It Possible to Teach Pre-service Language Teachers to Reflect?

I believe it is possible, and necessary, to teach pre-service language teachers to reflect. In fact, the operative word here is *teach* reflection, beyond the passing wonder of everyday commonsense reflections already mentioned in earlier chapters, which requires a systematic approach where teachers are trained in the practices and tools of reflection. This means that teacher educators should model and even articulate their own systematic reflections on their practice so that their students (i.e., pre-service teachers) can follow suit. It is necessary for pre-service teachers to learn the skills of reflection because engaging in RP is the best mechanism to become aware of what we actually do (teach) rather than what we think we do, and it lays good foundation for future professional development.

That said, novice teachers in training already have a full load of courses and other associated problems and issues to deal with in their teaching education programs.

I believe that reflecting is thinking and doing, and pre-service teachers who move from a dependence on the teacher trainer to reflection during their training will greatly benefit all through their careers but especially during their first year of teaching (Farrell, 2016a). Farrell (2016a) noted for example that a group of ESL teachers in their first year faced a dire situation of unreasonable workload demands such as unpaid marking, unpaid increased hours outside of school time on trips, lack of support from administration, large class sizes, and unorganized curricula; and without the help of a RP group to cope, all three would probably have quit teaching. RP can help to make the transition from teacher education programs to the first year smoother for novice ESL teachers because they are taught how to survive using the tools of reflection (see chapter 4).

There is growing research evidence within the field of language teacher education that encouraging language teachers, both pre-service and in-service, to engage in reflection is having a positive impact on their careers because teachers recognize the developmental value and transformative potential in reflective activities (Farrell, 2018a). Language teacher educators have various pedagogical tools at their disposal at the program and course level in order to encourage the habit of reflection – such as using technology, critical friendships, team teaching, peer coaching, dialogue, writing, action research, and analysis of critical incidents (as outlined earlier in this book) to encourage learner teachers to engage in reflective practice. In addition, language teacher educators must themselves be aware of the nature of reflection and the required attitudes that go along with becoming a reflective practitioner. It is not enough to encourage reflection though; language teacher educators themselves must model reflection by examining their own practices. I agree with Tony Wright (2010: 267) when he says that the goal of second language teacher education is to produce 'reflective teachers, in a process which involves socio-cognitive demands to introspect and collaborate with others, and which acknowledges previous learning and life experience as a starting point for new learning.'

Reflective Break

- Do you believe we can teach reflective practice to pre-service language teachers?
- Do you believe that we should teach reflective practice to pre-service language teachers?
- If your answers to the above questions are yes, how can this be accomplished?

Can Reflection Be Faked?

What a strange question to ask, you may think, but not really as it is very important to consider when many SLTE programs 'require' their teacher candidates 'to reflect.' What many SLTE programs are doing in fact is giving the appearance of implementing reflection in their programs and then pushing their teacher candidates into complying with the requirements to 'reflect' in the ways that the teacher educators define. Thus the appearance of complying becomes more important than the educational purpose of reflecting that leads to self-knowledge as a teacher. In many instances, teachers are required to 'produce' reflections on issues related to their teaching but in doing so they are instructed to follow ritualistic checklists that are presumed to promote reflection. As Roberts (1998: 59) has observed, when 'forced' to reflect, teacher candidates view reflection as an 'imposed course' requirement that has 'no real meaning for themselves.' What invariably happens is that many teacher candidates, because of the power differentials between teacher educators and themselves, will resort to giving the teacher educators what they want and this leads to 'faked' reflections.

It is important for teacher educators to engage pre-service teachers in experiences that develop the habit of reflective thinking. As Dewey (1933) noted, learning how to think begins with learning how to acquire the general habit of reflecting. In addition, it is important for teacher educators to define for themselves what they mean when telling their students to reflect. What is this reflection and how should it be accomplished and why? Teacher educators should allow time in their courses (preferably at the beginning) to define reflection and discuss with their teacher candidates what reflection is. For example, it is important for teacher educators to consider, when they encourage their teacher candidates to reflect, whose tradition this reflection is mirrored in. We must be cautious against hasty referencing (e.g., to Dewey, Schön, and/or Farrell) to legitimize any approach without a full understanding of the approach and its theoretical traditions. I would also suggest that teacher educators avoid reducing reflecting to recipe-following checklists and to promote reflection that considers teacher candidates' personal histories, their beliefs, theories, and expectations for practice which *may differ* from those of the teacher educators. This will lead to more productive reflections rather than faked reflections produced for a better grade (see also the question that follows on assessment of reflection).

Reflective Break

- Do you think it is possible to fake reflections?
- Have you ever faked your reflections?
- How can we move from the appearance of conducting reflections to more meaningful reflections?
- Do you think that teacher educators really understand what it means to reflect?
- Do you think that teacher educators reflect themselves?
- If your answer is no to the above question, should they reflect?

Is It Possible to Assess Reflection?

This is another important question that I get asked a lot and is linked to the above question on faking reflection. We must encourage our teacher candidates to reflect on *their* personal histories, beliefs, theories, and expectations for practice rather than follow our academic reflections as teacher educators. We need to ask whose needs are we taking into consideration: our needs as teacher educators or our teacher candidates' needs to grow and learn as language teachers? Indeed, we may want to consider not giving a grade, if we intend to promote productive reflection. I think it is very difficult to assess the quality of the reflection that takes place in teacher education, because if a teacher is reflecting on what he or she regards as critical, the results can only make any sense to the teacher concerned. Reflection also depends on the truthfulness of the pre-service teacher who is doing the reflection and how open-minded he or she is (see above about the importance of a reflective disposition). Some pre-service teachers have been socialized into the means of reporting and the discourse of reflection and give the teacher educator what he or she wants without any serious personal reflection. After all, pre-service teachers know that they are going to be graded and will give the educator whatever is required to pass the course. I believe this happens in every course but we must be on guard against the urge to produce grade grids or rubrics that tell a pre-service teacher what an 'A' grade in reflection is, because this really means that a teacher educator dictates the way and contents of reflections irrespective of the individual pre-service teacher or his or her personal experiences, prior knowledge, and characteristics – that are *different* from those of the teacher educator.

I believe we can assess certain aspects of reflection and this can be done if we want to consider different levels of reflection as outlined in chapter 1. For example,

Hatton & Smith (1995) described three progressive levels of reflection, with each increased level indicating more/better reflective processes: descriptive, dialogical, and critical reflection.

- *Descriptive reflection* involves reflecting on an event, activity, or problem with a simple description of the event without providing any reasons for the problem.
- *Dialogical reflection* is a more exploratory process and involves more inner dialogue where the teacher steps back to investigate why the event or problem happened and attempts to come up with various solutions.
- *Critical reflection* involves more meta-cognitive analysis where the teacher considers the wider socio-political context and moral judgment when examining the event, issue, or problem.

Yet another approach to assessment of reflection posited by Jay & Johnson (2002: 77–79) also identifies three progressive levels of reflection as follows:

- *Descriptive reflection* involves describing a situation or problem.
- *Comparative reflection* involves thinking about the situation for reflection from different perspectives. Teachers try to solve the problem while also questioning their values and beliefs.
- *Critical reflection* involves teachers looking at all the different perspectives of a situation/problem and all of the players involved: teachers, students, the school, and the community.

The above progressive level approach to assessing RP can be summarized in a three-level method that can be used in a general manner for assessing reflection.

- *Level 1*: The level of a teacher's actions in the classroom, or a teacher's observable behaviors. Of course this brings in the idea of someone having to decide which/what actions are 'good' and 'bad' or even observable. I discuss this issue in the section that follows.
- *Level 2*: The theoretical level, or the theories are behind the teacher's behaviors (observed in level 1). I would suggest that supervisors ask the teachers to outline their theories because there can be divergence between observed actions and the explained theory behind those actions. This is a good thing as it can generate lots of discussion about the teacher's teaching methods if the discussions are non-judgmental.
- *Level 3*: The ethical/moral level, or the role of the wider community in a teacher's theories (level 1) and practices (level 2). Some call this critical reflection, where teachers can be asked to consider what their overall roles are within the profession and the community in which they live.

I realize that the above levels are still somewhat ambiguous but I think they offer a general approach to assessing reflection. However I also believe that each educator must articulate the specific criteria that will be used to assess the quality of pre-service teachers' descriptive, dialogical, and/or critical reflection; I do not think that teachers should operate at any particular level other than the level that *they are ready* to reflect at. If they are not ready to reflect at the critical level, for example, then that is fine as long as they know what level they are at and the contents of their reflections. Teacher educators must be careful to avoid trying to 'push' teacher candidates to reflect at a particular level if they are not ready to reflect at that level because this will only lead to heightened (and unnecessary) anxiety associated with such 'forced' reflections. Teacher candidates should reflect on issues they find meaningful, and not what teacher educators think they should find meaningful. This of course means that again (see section above) the teacher educators and the pre-service teachers must come together and discuss what they all mean by 'reflection' and 'reflective practice' and what theoretical tradition they all want to follow when engaging in RP, rather than the educators just telling the teacher candidates to 'reflect'!

Another way to counteract the negative effects of assessing reflection is to encourage self-assessment, as I mentioned in the previous chapter, and have the teachers reflect on each of the five stages of Farrell's (2015b) framework and place the contents in a teaching portfolio for assessment. This would give teachers the necessary time and space to move at their own pace and also keep them away from any destructive over-critical tendencies that assessment can bring on. The real value of reflection for pre-service and in-service teachers is that the teacher is distancing him/herself from the event itself. This is important as teachers are sometimes too close emotionally to the class.

Reflective Break

- Should reflection be assessed?
- Do you think it is possible to assess reflection?
- How can reflection be best assessed?
- The 'level' approach to assessing reflection suggests that teachers reflect at three different levels: descriptive, conceptual, and critical. What level of reflection do you find yourself working at now? What does this mean to you as a reflective teacher?
- Do you think a teacher should operate (reflect) at any particular level?

Can Reflective Practice Be Used for Teacher Evaluation?

As discussed in the previous chapter, it is a fact of life that pre-service language teachers will be evaluated in some capacity over their careers, not just on how they reflect. Although each teacher evaluation may vary, the evaluation process invariably involves observations of some kind in the classroom by the supervisor who 'visits' or drops-in on one or more days to appraise 'features' of the pre-service language teacher's teaching behaviors. The 'features' (usually in terms of behaviors) to be desired (or otherwise) are often pre-determined by others (inside or outside the school) and presented as checkmarks on what is commonly called a teacher evaluation form.

Such approaches to pre-service language teacher evaluations have many shortcomings, as we have seen before: no agreement on what 'good' teaching is, rating of teaching behaviors is ambiguous, process is top-down. I will outline some of the shortcomings of such usual teacher evaluations and outline how reflection can be a more collaborative and beneficial to all parties concerned.

One immediate problem with evaluating teachers on 'good teaching' is that there is still no agreement on what 'good' means in all situations. Many times then, 'good' is based on preconceived opinions that may (or may not) be based on the most up-to-date development in research associated with the latest methods and approaches. For example, I have had the opportunity to observe pre-service language teachers in schools worldwide that still favor behaviorism and teacher-centered/controlled lessons; however, these same teachers are being trained in up-to-date developments that include more learner-centered approaches that are not considered 'good' by their supervisors.

This leads to another flaw with the usual approach to teacher evaluation: the scales that are used to rate specific activities teachers engage in. Many of these rating scales consist of some type of single (dichotomous) measure such as 'satisfactory' or 'needs improvement' or a rating scale that is numbered from 1 to 4 with one of these numbers more desirable than the other. Other popular scales have supervisors/observers rate teaching items as 'low', 'medium', or 'high'; or they are asked if they 'strongly agree', 'agree', are 'uncertain', 'disagree', 'strongly disagree', and so on. The problem here is that such rating lacks any precision (what is the difference between 'strongly agree' and 'agree' anyway?). This rating system leads to a lack of trust on the teachers' part; they tend not to trust administrators'/supervisors' ability to rate them; or worse, there may be perceptions of favoritism towards teachers who are more 'cooperative' in the school than others, regardless of their ability to teach. Indeed, some teachers have suggested that they believe that the real purpose of such evaluations is to find fault – what you are doing wrong in a 'gotcha' moment – rather than fair appraisal.

Such evaluations are conducted by a supervisor in a top-down, hierarchical process with the only evidence of teaching performance collected in the form of 'feedback'. Indeed, for the most part, the supervisor is the only one who takes notes, writes them up, and provides feedback on performance; this produces one-way communication, as the teacher is rarely asked to provide feedback about the process. The resulting evaluation is not really illuminating for the pre-service language teacher and I also suspect for the supervisor: the teacher does not find the process professionally rewarding and the supervisor does not really learn anything about the teacher.

So there is something of a standoff between the pre-service language teacher who is being evaluated and the supervisor who is evaluating, resulting in a culture of passivity and protection where many times teachers perform 'canned' lessons (i.e., they are coached and pre-prepared for evaluations) that try to reproduce many of the items on the checklist rather than actually teach the students at hand. In fact, many teachers have confided in me that they have used the *same* lesson for years with different supervisors when they know the day and time of the evaluation. Thus we can say with certainty that many current teacher evaluation systems have deficiencies, and the pre-service language teacher is separated from the act of teaching because he or she is being evaluated in terms of what he or she does rather than on who he or she is.

In order to rectify this standoff, we must consider two sides/views of the evaluation process: the pre-service language teacher's side and the supervisor's side. Many teachers maintain that evaluations are biased because they are conducted through a supervisor's subjective lens that rarely produces lasting professional effects for them as they continue their teaching. On the other side, many supervisors maintain that they are required to evaluate their teachers and that they feel this is somewhat of a burden for them because they realize that 'drop-in' classroom observations that require them to fill out a predetermined checklist may not reveal the overall true ability of the teacher being evaluated. Thus, teacher evaluation is considered onerous by both teachers who do not find it helpful to improve any aspects of their practice, and supervisors who find the process not very helpful when trying to gauge a teacher's overall performance. Teacher evaluations can be more collaborative, however, if both sides share the burden of evaluation and this can be encouraged if teachers are given more responsibility in the evaluation process – in other words, if we *shift* the burden of evaluation by requiring each teacher to compile a teaching portfolio, as outlined in a previous chapter.

A teacher portfolio for reflective and teacher evaluation purposes can act as a 'mirror' and as a 'map'. The portfolio as a 'mirror' allows teachers to 'see' their development in terms of their philosophy, principles, theory, practice, and beyond practice over time. The portfolio as a 'map' symbolizes creating a plan and setting goals for where teachers want to go in the future. Both 'mirror' and 'map' are excellent means for providing structure for pre-service language teachers who want to engage in self-reflection and self-assessment.

> **Reflective Break**
>
> • Do you believe reflection can be used for teacher evaluation?
> • Do you believe pre-service teachers should be involved in the evaluation process?

What Are Some of the Criticisms of Reflective Practice?

A number of scholars have urged caution as to the applicability of RP in education. Some may ask: if we get teachers to reflect, then what is the role of teacher educators? In addition, is this reflection supposed to focus only on practice? If reflection focuses only on practice I would suggest that this puts the teacher in a 'reflective practice bubble' because the person-as-teacher who is doing the reflection is not considered a part of the reflective process. When focusing only on practice, reflection is taken to be a fix-it tool to solve problems. Indeed, within TESOL, a recent review of the research on the practices that encourage TESOL teachers to reflection (Farrell, 2018a) discovered that the main focus of their reflections tended to be on issues related to classroom practices, but not much on themselves (philosophy) or beyond their classroom (critical reflection). Thus, Farrell (2015b) suggested that it may be an idea for teacher educators and TESOL teachers to be encouraged to expand their reflections on their philosophy so that they know who they are (teacher-as-person). They can also be encouraged to reflect beyond the classroom to include the greater socio-cultural context in which they find themselves teaching.

Important critical issues about reflective practice were also raised by Hatton & Smith (1995: 34–36) when they noted four key unresolved issues concerning reflective teaching:

- Is reflection limited to thought process about action, or more bound up in the action itself?

- Is reflection immediate and short term, or more extended and systematic? That is, what time frame is most suitable for reflective practice?
- Is reflection problem-centered, finding solutions to real classroom problems, or not? That is, should solving problems be an inherent characteristic of reflection? (Group discussion and journal writing are widely used as tools for reflection but they are not problem-solving.)
- How 'critical' does one get when reflecting? This refers to whether the one reflecting takes into account the wider political, cultural, and historical beliefs and values in finding solutions to problems.

Hatton & Smith (1995: 36) also see a number of 'barriers which hinder the achievement of reflective approaches':

- Reflection is not generally associated with working as a teacher; it is seen as a more academic exercise.
- Teachers need time and opportunity for development.
- Exposing oneself in a group of strangers can lead to vulnerability.
- The ideology of reflection is quite different than that of traditional approaches to teacher education.

In addition, reflection has also been criticized as being too individualistic a concept, as for example represented in the writings of Schön and others, and it is felt that collaboration should be emphasized more when discussing the implementation of the concept in teacher education programs. It is better for pre-service teachers to engage in reflection with others because they can offer different points of view that they would not necessarily achieve when reflecting alone, some scholars note.

It would be better for all teachers if they were able to share their reflections with others for their own professional development. Ways of sharing could include:

- Getting a group of teachers together to talk about teaching
- Collecting data from actual classroom teaching situations and sharing this data with the group for discussion by analyzing, evaluating, and interpreting the data in light of their unique context
- Self-observation with audio and/or video cameras; observation by group members for later group discussions
- Journal writing for reflection and comments by group members
- Taking on action research projects such as the teacher's pattern of questioning behavior
- Going to conferences and workshops, and subscribing to professional journals

All valid criticisms must be addressed by each teacher educator and teacher interested in adopting a reflective stance for their practice.

> **Reflective Break**
>
> - What are your answers to the criticisms raised in the section above?
> - Do you think reflection is more of an academic exercise rather than a practical activity for a teacher?
> - Do you think teachers should engage in teacher research and if so, what kind of research?

What Are the Benefits of Engaging in Reflective Practice?

In the previous sections I have outlined and discussed some of the criticisms of RP; now I outline and discuss some of its benefits. The first and most relevant benefit of teachers engaging in RP is that it helps free them from routine, as Dewey (1933) has noted. Although I think that a certain amount of routine is necessary and desirable for our students to be able to follow our lessons, language teachers must be careful about falling into a trap of routine that lulls them into a type of boring rhythm that can stupefy their creativity as teachers. This can happen easily in following a textbook exactly as it is outlined because such books are designed to produce lessons in each chapter that are similar (if not the same) and the 'teacher's book' is designed to produce 'teacher-proof lessons' or lessons that do not deviate from the textbook. While some learning will inevitably take place, it does so in spite of the teacher's presence because the teacher just hums along to the textbook tune. Language teachers in my view teach students and not textbooks, and the best teachers manipulate such textbooks so that their lessons are creative and dynamic and thus provide more opportunities for their students to learn.

Engaging in RP allows teachers to act in a deliberate, intentional manner and avoid the 'I don't know what I will do today' syndrome. Teachers act deliberately because they notice something is happening in their lesson as their students react or do not react in a particular manner. They must ask themselves such questions about their teaching as: is the dog wagging the tail, or is the tail wagging the dog – in other words, am I teaching the lesson or not. Teachers are active decision-makers and as such they 'wag the tail' of their teaching as they are directing their lessons and providing as many opportunities as possible for their students to learn.

Teachers can learn from engaging in RP if they cultivate a reflective disposition to be open to learning and noticing what is happening. By engaging in RP, language teachers can look at their experiences in a systematic manner and use the information gained from this to make changes if necessary, cognitively and/or behaviorally, and as a result obtain growth as a teacher. As Dewey (1933: 87) has noted, growth comes from a 'reconstruction of experience', so by reflecting on our own experiences we can reconstruct our own educational perspective. Reflective practice enables language teachers to notice what is happening in each lesson and make connections across and between lessons so that they have full comprehension of their practice. As a result, RP can be a transformative experience for language teachers because such noticing allows for deeper knowledge that enables such transformative learning.

Although I have focused on the professional benefits from reflecting on practice for language teachers, there are also personal benefits such as noticing what is going on around you in your daily life rather than what you think is going on. In other words, reflecting can lead us to become more realistic about what is going well because of the evidence we notice, and avoid falling into the trap of becoming negative without sufficient evidence of such negativity. Rather than evading issues, we can use our skills of reflection to research them and look for evidence so that we can make informed decisions about how we will deal with them in the future. As Schön has noted (in Osterman & Kottkamp, 1993: 54):

> When a practitioner becomes a researcher into his [or her] practice, he [or she] engages in a continuing process of self-education ... the recognition of error, with its resulting uncertainty, can become a source of discovery rather than an occasion for self-defense.

Engaging in RP has benefits beyond teaching, such as a deeper understanding of who you are as a person, your personal values, and that others around you may have different values. In such a manner, everyday reflective practice allows us to grow as human beings so that we are proactive in all our endeavors. As I mentioned in chapter 3, principle 6, RP is a way of life and can free us from negativity so that we can become more mindful human beings.

Reflective Break

- What benefits can you think of as a result of engaging in reflective practice?
- Are you aware of any routines in your teaching?
- How can engaging in reflective practice break teaching routines?
- Do you think reflection can have benefits beyond teaching?
- If yes, what benefits?

What Is the Future for Reflective Practice?

When we talk about reflection and RP, too often this is of an implicit nature in terms of how we define these concepts. Some think that RP means teachers struggling to articulate their internal thoughts about teaching, while others think it is concerned with how teachers feel about how a lesson went without much evidence documenting what actually occurred. Such thoughts can be demoralizing because teachers may focus on what they think is the negative rather than what may have happened which in fact was positive. So, teachers and teacher educators should define what they mean by engaging in reflection and RP, and some of these definitions should at the very least involve teachers gathering evidence or data about their practices both inside and outside the classroom in their particular context and then sharing (through dialogue and/or writing) what they discover with other teachers, so that RP is more social than individual.

In addition, although I have mentioned this above, within teacher education some wonder how RP can be assessed; they feel that if it cannot, it should be dismissed. I believe that such debate limits reflection and returns it back to the idea of technical rationality that it was designed against – we may be replacing one set of checklists with another. Yes, we must be on guard against superficial reflections but we must also be on guard against instituting recipe-following checklists that teachers 'reflect with compliantly' just to satisfy some teacher educator's need rather than their own need to question and challenge practice. As I have already stressed, RP is a means for promoting critical reflection rather than another educational tool that is used to exercise control and follow established conventions, which is not productive or developmental for anyone involved.

'Productive reflection' (Cressey et al., 2006) is contextualized and involves individuals reflecting on their practices in the company of other professionals. In such a manner, organizations such as schools (see chapter 6 on cultivating reflection in the workplace) should be involved because teachers do not work in isolation; rather they work in a community that includes students, teachers, administrators, and the outside community. All should be involved in the reflective process in the shared interests of the wider group/community. The results of such productive reflections are to generate new possibilities for the group as a whole as well as the individuals who are reflecting within the group. In addition, one of the qualities of productive reflection that is identified by Cressey et al. (2006: 22) is that reflection is a dynamic, 'open, unpredictable process' that changes over time. Thus language teachers who engage in reflection and RP must develop a tolerance for ambiguity and as a result also develop a reflective disposition of open-mindedness, responsibility, and wholeheartedness so that they can acquire the resourcefulness and resilience necessary to face any future challenges and changes in their careers.

I have been working with the concept of reflection and RP for a long time and I have not been a fan of the different theoretical approaches if they have not led to any tangible uses for teachers in the frontlines. The reason for this is I was a teacher first and foremost before I became a teacher educator, and so I have always attempted to bring the teacher's voice into the discussions of RP. I agree with Polanyi (1967) when he noted that teachers know more than they can tell, their deep tacit knowledge, and this knowledge is valuable. RP can help teachers articulate this knowledge to themselves and others so that they can provide more learning opportunities for their students. However, it is important to reiterate, we must be careful of treating reflection as a task that ticks some administrator's box where observers already have preconceived notions about what teachers *should* reflect on.

We must constantly define what we mean by reflection and make sure that teachers are front and central of the process. Yes, as this chapter has pointed out in an anticipator reflective mode, there still are a lot of questions we can ask about reflection and RP (e,g., about definitions, typologies, principles, tools, etc.) and this is a good thing. However, because differences abound as to what reflection is and how it should be operationalized, perhaps it is the task of each teacher educator, teacher, and every other stakeholder to try to answer these questions so that they will be able to decide for themselves how to encourage and influence reflection as well as what outcomes they expect. I would suggest that there are commonalities within and across different approaches, typologies, and definitions of RP that we can agree on; for example, it is a cognitive process that requires some kind of action on the part of the person reflecting. In addition, reflection can be a response to a puzzling issue, or a practitioner can embark on reflection out of curiosity as to his or her assumptions, beliefs, values, theories, and practices related to teaching.

Most, if not all models, include the importance of contextual factors even if individuals are reflecting alone, because the context plays an important role in the nature and outcomes of reflection. I would also suggest that most approaches encourage practitioners to plan what to do, to collect information regarding the issue of interest before taking any action on the matter, and then to act based on the information obtained by the whole reflective process. The action that is to be taken should also be structured in some manner, as espoused in many of the approaches/typologies. However, the 'level' of structuring differs in many approaches/typologies depending on the nature of the model and its series of levels or iterations. For example, in the framework for reflecting on practice that I developed, teachers are encouraged to reflect through five stages or levels that encompass many of the other models'/approaches'/typologies' levels or iterations.

Some models consider that there is a developmental process to reflection that moves through three (although some models have seven) different levels of reflective thinking, from an initial descriptive reflection level to conceptual reflection to critical reflection, with different definitions of each. Some scholars suggest that the iterative process involved in reflection is necessary if we want to move teachers from descriptive to critical or from surface reflection to deep reflection, because they consider descriptive reflection as 'non-reflective' thinking. However, I do not agree that descriptive reflection is 'non-reflective' thinking and I would caution against the desire to try to 'push' any teacher to move to a different level until he or she is ready to reflect at that level, given that novice teachers are still considering their repertoire of teaching skills in the classroom. This of course brings back the issues with assessment and reflection for novice teachers as discussed before, but this further highlights the need for self-assessment through reflection rather than a 'one-size-fits-all' approach to teacher evaluation.

Reflective Break

- What do you think is the future for reflective practice?
- If language teacher education programs identify reflection as a key component of prospective teacher professional preparation, how do you think these programs should incorporate reflective practice?

Final Reflections: The Equinox Series Reflective Practice in Language Education

The series **Reflective Practice in Language Education** (https://www.equinoxpub.com/home/reflective-practice-language-education/) covers different issues related to RP in language education and begins with this book that introduces these areas. The other titles in the series will clarify the different approaches that have been taken within RP and outline current themes that have emerged in the research on various topics and methods of reflection that have occurred.

The recent surge in popularity of the concept of RP in many professions is a good indicator that it has taken hold beyond the usual bandwagon movements (see above) that we sometimes come across with the introduction of new concepts. Within language education RP has become very popular not only from an academic point of view and a research perspective but also in terms of practical usage by language teachers. Every university is involved with this concept in some way at the moment, and it is popular in faculties of Education, Humanities, and

Social Sciences, from English departments to Education departments to Applied Linguistics and teaching English to speakers of other languages (TESOL) departments. So there is a definite need for such practice-oriented books on RP which all of these stakeholders can pick up and use. It is this need that the present series aims to address.

Here are some of the forthcoming titles:

- *Using video to support teacher reflection and development* by Laura Baecher and Steve Mann. This book aims to review and detail digital video use in the field of language teacher education, while also reviewing its use in other fields of education (e.g., maths teaching, health care). The book will draw on a growing community of teacher educators and feature some of their experiences and views (through data and vignettes). In doing so, the book will help to share innovative and effective video and visual media use in language teacher education. This will enable reflection and further methodological development on areas of focus such as webinars, stimulated recall, video in peer observation, flipped training content, screen-capture feedback, video-editing and analysis, captioning tools, and video for mentoring. Video helps engage teacher learners in noticing and learning in complex situations. It is thus particularly well suited for supporting novice teachers' learning.

- *English language teacher beliefs* by Farahnaz Faez and Michael Karas. This book will focus on understanding teachers' beliefs in connection with (reflective) practice. Teaching is a multi-faceted, cognitively demanding profession that requires teachers to make active decisions. Teachers cannot simply 'go through the motions' of teaching and implement prescribed strategies; they must have attuned understandings of both their contexts and themselves as teachers in order to effectively instruct in the classroom. A key component of this understanding is intertwined with reflective practice. This book will be based in practice. Drawing on Farrell's (2015b) framework for RP, it will outline the notion of teacher beliefs along with specific strategies as to how teachers can use RP to understand their beliefs. This book will delve deeply into the various types of beliefs, which include, but are not limited to: general beliefs about teaching and learning; English language teaching beliefs; specific beliefs about various pedagogical strategies; the nature of knowledge itself; teachers' beliefs about their own capabilities (i.e., self-efficacy). This book will be a useful tool for all English language teachers and/or teacher educators, but especially useful for teachers who have engaged in the 'border-crossing' nature of ELT. TESOL is a global profession; teachers travel to different countries to teach, and prospective teachers often go overseas for teacher preparation. Teaching, or learning to teach, in a foreign context complicates matters further as teachers must come to terms with their own beliefs, but also a new professional context. This book will explicitly address these challenges.

- ***The reflective cycle of the teaching practicum*** by Fiona Farr and Angela Farrell. This book has a focus on the practice cycle, or practicum, of ELT education programs. Practice teaching is a key component of all good ELTE programs, and provides a forum for novice teachers to begin to cross the theory/practice divide in a way which allows them to try out ideas in a classroom setting. This typically happens after a period of theoretical induction and the observation of more experienced teachers, and can often begin in a very scaffolded way through micro or team teaching, before moving to more independence. At all stages of this practice-oriented process, reflection is a fundamental and obligatory underlying principle, the integration of which leads to informed decisions on change implementation to improve teaching. This book will begin with a theoretical and research-informed introduction to both reflective practice and the practicum, followed by definitions and typologies. Various tools and sources of evidence to support the reflective process during the practicum will be investigated, using many data-rich examples from our own and others' professional contexts over a number of years. These will be applied to observation of more experienced teachers and self-observation of one's own practice as facilitators of informed decisions for change. The process of reflection as a life-long developmental practice will be explored as the book concludes.

- ***Micro-reflection on classroom communication: A FAB framework*** by Hansun Zhang Waring and Sarah Chepkirui Creider. Traditional concerns with classroom communication have centered on questions such as: who talks more, whether the interaction is teacher-centered or student-centered, whether participation is restricted to a few or available to all, what kinds of questions teachers ask (display or referential), and what kinds of feedback they give. These indicators provide a simple and useful way of capturing classroom communication in distributional and categorical terms. Less attention has been devoted to observing and understanding the quality of this communication – whether it facilitates learning regardless of, for example, who talks more. Based on over a decade of fine-grained analysis of video-recorded ESL classroom interaction, this book offers one way of seeing and gauging the quality of classroom communication beyond distributions and categories. In particular, by parsing detailed transcripts of actual classroom interaction, it invites reflective conversations on how three principles of skillful classroom communication may be practiced in the micro-moments of classroom interaction: (1) fostering an inviting classroom environment, (2) attending to student voices, and (3) balancing competing demands (FAB). Attention to the moment-by-moment complexity of the classroom also allows teachers to learn and practice the skill of noticing, the first step in an iterative cycle of noticing, reflecting, and practicing. That is, along with reflecting on what happened in a classroom, teachers must also learn to notice what is happening in the moment. The goal is to cultivate a mentality of micro-reflection – one that sensitizes teachers to the consequentiality of every move they make in the simultaneity and sequentiality of second-by-second classroom interaction.

- *Surviving the Induction Years of Language Teaching: The Importance of Reflective Practice* by Thomas S. C. Farrell. *Should I stay or should I go?* Anecdotal evidence suggests that this rhetorical question may be prevalent for many early-career teachers to ask themselves after their first few years of teaching English to speakers of other languages (TESOL). Early-career teachers include novice teachers after their first year and especially in their third year of teaching. Of those ESL teachers who survive their first year (for more on this, see Farrell, 2016a) research has noted that the first-year 'transition traumas' can have serious repercussions on their motivation and commitment in the following years and in many cases have led to unacceptably high levels of early career teacher attrition globally. This book is unique to the language teaching profession because it outlines the detailed experiences of one ESL teacher during his first year and then during his third year to see what challenges he encountered during these important novice years. It is important for teacher-educators, teachers, and administrators to understand what early-career teachers experience so that they can better be supported to continue in the profession for many more years to come. The results of this analysis will lead to the development of a comprehensive framework for the professional development of novice teachers through RP that is grounded in the classroom realities of real teaching contexts so that they can develop beyond their novice years and become expert ESL teachers. In addition, the suggestions presented in this book can be operationalized as standards for future ESL/EFL teacher education and development programs worldwide.

These five books, along with the current one written as an introduction to RP for language educators, I believe will enlighten and inform us all so that we can continue to provide the best learning opportunities for all our students. Happy reflecting!

References

Ahmadi, P., Samad, A. A., & Noordin, N. (2013). Identity formation of TEFL graduate students through oral discourse socialization. *Theory and Practice in Language Studies*, 3(10), 1764–1769.

Akbari, R. (2007). Reflections on reflection: A critical appraisal of reflective practices in L2 teacher education. *System*, 35(2), 192–207.
https://doi.org/10.1016/j.system.2006.12.008

Argyris, C., & Schön, D. (1974). *Theory in practice: Increasing professional effectiveness*. San Francisco: Jossey Bass.

Argyris, C., & Schön, D. (1978). *Organizational learning: A theory of action perspective*. Reading, MA: Addison Wesley.

Banegas, D., Pavese, A., Velázquez, A., & Vélez, S. M. (2013). Teacher professional development through collaborative action research: Impact on foreign English-language teaching and learning. *Educational Action Research*, 21(2), 185–201.
https://doi.org/10.1080/09650792.2013.789717

Barkhuizen, G., & Wette, R. (2008). Narrative frames for investigating the experiences of language teachers. *System*, 36(3), 372–387.
https://doi.org/10.1016/j.system.2008.02.002

Bartlett, L. (1990). Teacher development through reflective teaching. In J. C. Richards, & D. Nunan (eds.), *Second language teacher education* (pp. 202–214). New York: Cambridge University Press.

Borton, T. (1970). *Reach, teach and touch*. London: McGraw Hill.

Boud, D., Keogh, R., & Walker, D. (eds.) (1985). *Reflection: Turning experience into learning*. New York: Kogan Page Ltd.

Brookfield, S. D. (1995). *Becoming a critically reflective teacher*. San Fransisco: Jossey-Bass.

Burns, A., & Richards. J. C. (eds.) (2009). *The Cambridge guide to second language teacher education*. New York: Cambridge University Press.

Calderhead, J. (1989). Reflective teaching and teacher education. *Teaching and Teacher Education*, 5(1), 43–51. https://doi.org/10.1016/0742-051X(89)90018-8

Carper, B. (1978). Fundamental patterns of knowing in nursing. *Advances in Nursing Science*, 1(1), 13–23. https://doi.org/10.1097/00012272-197810000-00004

Chi, F. (2013). Turning experiences into critical reflections: Examples from Taiwanese in-service teachers. *Asia-Pacific Journal of Teacher Education*, 41(1), 28–40. https://doi.org/10.1080/1359866X.2012.753987

Chien, C. (2013). Analysis of a language teacher's journal of classroom practice as reflective practice. *Reflective Practice*, 14(1), 131–143. https://doi.org/10.1080/14623943.2012.732951

Clarke, A. (1995). Professional development in practicum settings: Reflective practice under scrutiny. *Teaching and Teacher Education*, 11, 243–261. https://doi.org/10.1016/0742-051X(94)00028-5

Clarke, M. (1982). The dysfunctions of the theory/practice discourse. *TESOL Quarterly*, 28(1), 9–26.

Collin, S., Karsenti, T., & Komis, V. (2013). Reflective practice in initial teacher training: Critiques and perspectives. *Reflective Practice*, 14(1), 104–117. https://doi.org/10.1080/14623943.2012.732935

Copeland, W. D., Birmingham, C., De La Cruz, E., & Lewin, B. (1993). The reflective practitioner in teaching: Toward a research agenda. *Teaching and Teacher Education*, 9(4), 347–359. https://doi.org/10.1016/0742-051X(93)90002-X

Cressey, P., Boud, D., & Docherty, P. (2006). The emergence of productive reflection. In D. Boud, P. Cressey, & P. Docherty (eds.), *Productive reflection at work: Learning for changing organizations* (pp. 10–26). London: Routledge.

Crooks, G. (2013). *Critical ELT in action: Foundations, promises, praxis.* New York: Routledge. https://doi.org/10.4324/9780203844250

Cruickshank, D., & Applegate, J. (1981). Reflective teaching as a strategy for teacher growth. *Educational Leadership*, 38, 553–554.

Day, C. (1993). Reflection: A necessary but not sufficient condition for teacher development. *British Educational Research Journal*, 19, 83–93. https://doi.org/10.1080/0141192930190107

Day, R. R. (2013). Peer observation and reflection in the ELT practicum. *International Journal of Literature and Language Education*, 52, 1–8.

Dewey, J. (1910/1933). *How we think: A restatement of the relation of reflective thinking to the educative process.* Boston: Houghton-Mifflin. https://doi.org/10.1037/10903-000

Dooly, M., & Sadler, R. (2013). Filling in the gaps: Linking theory and practice through telecollaboration in teacher education. *Recall*, 25(1), 4–29. https://doi.org/10.1017/S0958344012000237

Ecclestone, K. (1996). The reflective practitioner: Mantra or model for emancipation? *Studies in the Education of Adults*, 28(2), 146–161. https://doi.org/10.1080/02660830.1996.11730637

Fanselow, J. F. (1988). 'Let's see': Contrasting conversations about teaching. *TESOL Quarterly*, 22, 113–130. https://doi.org/10.2307/3587064

Farrell, T. S. C. (1999). Teachers talking about teaching: Creating conditions for reflection. *TESL-EJ*, 4(2), 1–17.

Farrell, T. S. C. (2003). Learning to teach English language during the first year: Personal influences and challenges. *Teaching and Teacher Education*, 19(1), 95–111. https://doi.org/10.1016/S0742-051X(02)00088-4

Farrell, T. S. C. (2004). *Reflective practice in action: 80 reflection breaks for busy teachers.* Thousand Oaks, CA: Corwin Press.

Farrell, T. S. C. (2007a). Failing the practicum: Narrowing the gap between expectations and reality with reflective practice. *TESOL Quarterly*, 41(1), 193–201. https://doi.org/10.1002/j.1545-7249.2007.tb00049.x

Farrell, T. S. C. (2007b). *Reflective language teaching: From research to practice.* London: Continuum Press.

Farrell, T. S. C. (2008). *Novice language teachers: Insights and perspectives for the first year.* London: Equinox.

Farrell, T. S. C. (2009). Critical reflection in a TESL course: Mapping conceptual change. *ELT Journal*, 63(3), 221–229. https://doi.org/10.1093/elt/ccn058

Farrell, T. S. C. (2011). Exploring the professional role identities of experienced ESL teachers through reflective practice. *System*, 39(1), 54–62. https://doi.org/10.1016/j.system.2011.01.012

Farrell, T. S. C. (2012a). Reflecting on reflective practice: (Re)visiting Dewey and Schön. *TESOL Journal*, 3(1), 7–16. https://doi.org/10.1002/tesj.10

Farrell, T. S. C. (2012b). *Reflecting on teaching the four skills: 60 strategies for professional development.* Ann Arbor: The University of Michigan Press. https://doi.org/10.3998/mpub.4745438

Farrell, T. S. C. (2012c). Novice-service language teacher development: Bridging the gap between preservice and in-service education and development. *TESOL Quarterly*, 46(3), 435–449. https://doi.org/10.1002/tesq.36

Farrell, T. S. C. (2013a). *Reflective practice in ESL teacher development groups: From practices to principles.* Basingstoke, UK: Palgrave Macmillan. https://doi.org/10.1057/9781137317193

Farrell, T. S. C. (2013b). *Reflective writing for language teachers.* Sheffield, UK: Equinox Publishing Ltd.

Farrell, T. S. C. (2013c). Reflecting on ESL teacher expertise: A case study. *System*, 41(4), 1070–1082. https://doi.org/10.1016/j.system.2013.10.014

Farrell, T. S. C. (2014). 'I've plateaued…gone a little stale.' Mid-career reflections in a teacher reflection group. *Reflective Practice*, 15(4), 504–517. https://doi.org/10.1080/14623943.2014.900029

Farrell, T. S. C. (ed.) (2015a). *International perspectives on English language teacher education: Innovations from the field.* Basingstoke, UK: Palgrave Macmillan. https://doi.org/10.1057/9781137440068

Farrell, T. S. C. (2015b). *Promoting teacher reflection in second language education: A framework for TESOL professionals.* New York: Routledge.

Farrell, T. S. C. (2015c). It's not *who* you are! It's *how* you teach! Critical competencies associated with effective teaching. *RELC Journal*, 46(1), 79–88. https://doi.org/10.1177/0033688214568096

Farrell, T. S. C. (2016a). *From trainee to teacher: Reflective practice for novice teachers.* Sheffield, UK: Equinox.

Farrell, T. S. C. (2016b). The practices of encouraging TESOL teachers to engage in reflective practice: An appraisal of recent research contributions. *Language Teaching Research*, 20(2), 223–247. https://doi.org/10.1177/1362168815617335

Farrell, T. S. C. (2016c). TESOL, a profession that eats its young! The importance of reflective practice in language teacher education. *Iranian Journal of Language Teaching Research*, 4(3), 97–107.

Farrell, T. S. C. (2016d). Surviving the transition shock in the first year of teaching through reflective practice. *System*, 61(3), 12–19. https://doi.org/10.1016/j.system.2016.07.005

Farrell, T. S. C. (2016e). The teacher is a facilitator: Reflecting on ESL teacher beliefs through metaphor analysis. *Iranian Journal of Language Teaching Research*, 4(1), 1–10.

Farrell, T. S. C. (2017). 'Who I am is how I teach': Reflecting on teacher role identity. In G. Barkhuizen (ed.), *Reflections on language teacher identity research* (pp. 183–189). London: Routledge.

Farrell, T. S. C. (2018a). *Research on reflective practice in TESOL.* New York: Routledge.

Farrell, T. S. C. (2018b). *Reflective language teaching: Practical applications for TESOL teachers* (2nd Edition). London: Bloomsbury.

Farrell, T. S. C., & Baecher, L. (2017). *Reflecting on critical incidents in language education.* London: Bloomsbury.

Farrell, T. S. C., & Bennis, K. (2013). Reflecting on ESL teacher beliefs and classroom practices: A case study. *RELC Journal*, 44, 163–176. https://doi.org/10.1177/0033688213488463

Farrell, T. S. C., & Ives, J. (2015). Exploring teacher beliefs and classroom practices through reflective practice. *Language Teaching Research*, 19(5), 594–610. https://doi.org/10.1177/1362168814541722

Farrell, T. S. C., & Jacobs, G. (2016). Practicing what we preach: Teacher reflection groups on cooperative learning. *TESL-EJ*, 19(4), February.

Farrell, T. S. C., & Kennedy, B. (2019). A reflective practice framework for TESOL teachers: One teacher's reflective journey. *Reflective Practice*, 20(1), 1–12.

Farrell, T. S. C., & Mom, V. (2015). Exploring teacher questions through reflective practice. *Reflective Practice*, 16(6), 849–866. https://doi.org/10.1080/14623943.2015.1095734

Farrell, T. S. C., & Vos, R (2018). Exploring the principles and practices of teaching L2 speaking: Importance of reflective practice. *IJLTR*, 4(3), 97–107.

Farrell, T. S. C., & Yang, D. (2017). Exploring an EAP teacher's beliefs and practices in teaching L2 speaking: A case study. *RELC Journal*, published online September 26. https://doi.org/10.1177/0033688217730144

Feiman-Nemser, S., & Floden, R. (1986). The cultures of teaching. In M. C. Wittrock (ed.), *Handbook of research on teaching* (pp. 505–525). New York: Macmillan.

Freeman, D. (2016). *Educating second language teachers.* Oxford: Oxford University Press.

Freese, A. R. (1999). The role of reflection on preservice teachers' development in the context of a professional development school. *Teaching and Teacher Education*, 15(8), 895–909. https://doi.org/10.1016/S0742-051X(99)00029-3

Genc, Z. S. (2010). Teacher autonomy through reflective journals among teachers of English as a foreign language in Turkey. *Teacher Development*, 14(3), 397–409. https://doi.org/10.1080/13664530.2010.504028

Gibbs, G. (1988). *Learning by doing: A guide to teaching and learning methods.* Oxford: Further Education Unit Oxford Polytechnic.

Grimmett, P., Mackinnon, A., Erickson, G., & Riecken, T. (1990). Reflective practice in teacher education. In R. Clift, W. Houston, and M. Pugach (eds.). *Encouraging reflective practice in education: An analysis of issues and programs.* New York: Teachers College Press.

Hatton, N., & Smith, D. (1995). Reflection in teacher education: Towards definition and implementation. *Teaching and Teacher Education*, 11(1), 33–49. https://doi.org/10.1016/0742-051X(94)00012-U

Hooks, B. (1994). *Teaching to transgress: Education as the practice of freedom.* New York: Routledge.

Hung, H., & Yeh, H. (2013). Forming a change environment to encourage professional development through a teacher study group. *Teaching & Teacher Education*, 36, 153–165.

Jay, J. K., & Johnson, K. L. (2002). Capturing complexity: A typology of reflective practice for teacher education. *Teaching and Teacher Education*, 18(1), 73–85. https://doi.org/10.1016/S0742-051X(01)00051-8

Johns, C. (1995). Framing learning through reflection within Carper's fundamental ways of knowing in nursing. *Journal of Advanced Nursing*, 22(2), 226–234. https://doi.org/10.1046/j.1365-2648.1995.22020226.x

Kemmis, S. (1985). Action research and the politics of reflection. In D. Boud, R. Keogh, & D. Walker (eds.). *Reflection: Turning experience into learning* (pp. 139–163). New York: Kogan Page Ltd.

Kemmis, S., & McTaggart, R. (1988). *The action research planner* (3rd Edition). Geelong, Australia: Deakin University Press.

Knezedivc, B. (2001). Action research. *IATEFL Teacher Development SIG Newsletter*, 1, 10–12.

Kolb, D. A. (1984). *Experiential learning: Experience as the source of learning and development.* Englewood Cliffs, NJ: Prentice-Hall, Inc.

Kolb, D. A. & Fry, R. E. (1975). Toward an applied theory of experiential learning. In C. Cooper (ed.), *Theories of group processes.* New York: John Wiley & Sons.

Korthagen, F. (1985). Reflective teaching and preservice teacher education in the Netherlands. *Journal of Teacher Education*, 36(5), 11–15. https://doi.org/10.1177/002248718503600502

Korthagen, F. (1993). Two modes of reflection. *Teaching and Teacher Education*, 9(3), 317–326. https://doi.org/10.1016/0742-051X(93)90046-J

Korthagen, F., & Wubbels, T. (1995). Characteristics of reflective practitioners: Towards an operationalization of the concept of reflection. *Teachers and Teaching: Theory and Practice*, 1(1), 51–72. https://doi.org/10.1080/1354060950010105

Kumaravadivelu, B. (2003). *Beyond methods: Macrostrategies for language teaching*. New Haven, CT: Yale University Press.

Kumaravadivelu, B. (2012). *Language teacher education for a global society*. New York: Routledge. https://doi.org/10.4324/9780203832530

Lakshmi, B. S. (2014). Reflective practice through journal writing and peer observation: A case study. *Turkish Online Journal of Distance Education*, 15(4), 189–204. https://doi.org/10.17718/tojde.21757

Larrivee, B. (2000). Transforming teaching practice: Becoming the critically reflective teacher. *Reflective Practice*, 1(3), 293–307. https://doi.org/10.1080/713693162

Lortie, D. C. (1975). *Schoolteacher: A sociological study*. Chicago: University of Chicago Press.

Loughran, J. (2002). Effective reflective practice: In search of meaning in learning about teaching. *Journal of Teacher Education*, 53(1), 33–43. https://doi.org/10.1177/0022487102053001004

Lyons, N. (1998). Reflection in teaching: Can it be developmental? A portfolio perspective. *Teacher Education Quarterly*, 25(1), 115–127.

Malderez, A. & Bodoczky, C. (1999). *Mentor courses: A resource book for trainer trainers*. Cambridge: Cambridge University Press.

Mann, S., & Walsh, S. (2013). RP or 'RIP': A critical perspective on reflective practice. *Applied Linguistics Review*, 4(2), 291–315. https://doi.org/10.1515/applirev-2013-0013

Mann, S., & Walsh, S. (2017). *Reflective practice in English language teaching*. New York: Routledge. https://doi.org/10.4324/9781315733395

McFee, G. (1993). Reflections on the nature of action-research. *Cambridge Journal of Education*, 23, 173–183. https://doi.org/10.1080/0305764930230205

Mergendoller, R., & Sacks, C. (1994). Concerning the relationship between teachers' theoretical orientations toward reading and their concept maps. *Teaching and Teacher Education*, 10, 589–599. https://doi.org/10.1016/0742-051X(94)90028-0

Mezirow, J. (1998). On critical reflection. *Adult Education Quarterly*, 48(3), 185–198. https://doi.org/10.1177/074171369804800305

Miles, S., Barrett, E., Barton, L., Furlong, J., Galvin, C., & Whitty, G. (1993). Initial teacher education in England and Wales: A topography. *Research Papers in Education*, 8(3), 275–304.

Oberg, A., & Blades, C. (1990). The spoken and the unspoken: The story of an educator. *Phenomonology+Pedagogy*, 8, 161–180.

Orland-Barak, L. (2005). Portfolios as evidence of reflective practice: What remains 'untold'. *Educational Research*, 47(1), 25–44. https://doi.org/10.1080/0013188042000337541

Osterman, K. F., & Kottkamp, R. B. (1993). *Reflective practice for educators*. Thousand Oaks, CA: Corwin.

Palmer, P. J. (1998). *The courage to teach*. San Francisco: Jossey-Bass.

Parra, M., Gutiérrez, R., & Aldana, M. (2015). Engaging in critically reflective teaching: From theory to practice in pursuit of transformative learning. *Reflective Practice*, 16(1), 16–30. https://doi.org/10.1080/14623943.2014.944141

Polanyi, M. (1967). *The tacit dimension*. Chicago: The University of Chicago Press.

Richards, J. C., & Farrell, T. S. C. (2005). *Professional development for language teachers*. New York: Cambridge University Press. https://doi.org/10.1017/CBO9780511667237

Richards, J. C., & Lockhard, C. (1994). *Reflective teaching*. New York: Cambridge University Press.

Roberts, J. (1998). *Second language teacher education*. London: Arnold.

Rodgers, C. R. (2002). Defining reflection: Another look at John Dewey and reflective thinking. *Teachers College Record*, 104(4), 842–866. https://doi.org/10.1111/1467-9620.00181

Rolfe, G., Freshwater, D., & Jasper, M. (2001). *Critical reflection in nursing and the helping professions: A user's guide*. Basingstoke, UK: Palgrave Macmillan.

Schön, D. A. (1983). *The reflective practitioner: How professionals think in action*. New York: Basic Books.

Schön, D. (1987). *Educating the reflective practitioner*. San Francisco: Jossey-Bass.

Shapiro, S. B., & Reiff, J. (1993). A framework for reflective inquiry on practice: Beyond intuition and experience. *Psychological Reports*, 73, 1379–1394. https://doi.org/10.2466/pr0.1993.73.3f.1379

Shelley, M., Murphy, L., & White, C. J. (2013). Language teacher development in a narrative frame: The transition from classroom to distance and blended settings. *System*, 41(3), 560–574. https://doi.org/10.1016/j.system.2013.06.002

Shi, L., & Yang, L. (2014). A community of practice of teaching English writing in a Chinese university. *System*, 42, 133–142. https://doi.org/10.1016/j.system.2013.11.009

Shoffner, M. (2008). Informal reflection in pre-service education. *Reflective Practice*, 9(2), 123–134. https://doi.org/10.1080/14623940802005392

Shulman, J. (ed.). (1992). *Case methods in teacher education*. New York: Teachers College Press.

Smyth, J. (1989). Developing and sustaining critical reflection in teacher education. *Journal of Teacher Education*, 40(2), 2–9. https://doi.org/10.1177/002248718904000202

Stanley, C. (1998). A framework for teacher reflectivity. *TESOL Quarterly*, 32, 584–591. https://doi.org/10.2307/3588129

Tabachnik, R., & Zeichner, K. (2002). Reflections on reflective teaching. In A. Pollard. (ed.), *Readings for reflective teaching* (pp. 13–16). London: Continuum.

Taggart, G., & Wilson, A. P. (1998). *Promoting reflective thinking in teachers*. Thousand Oaks, CA: Corwin Press.

Tremmel, R. (1993). Zen and the art of reflective practice in teacher education. *Harvard Educational Review*, 63(4), 434–458. https://doi.org/10.17763/haer.63.4.m42704n778561176

Urzúa, A., & Vásquez, C. (2008). Reflection and professional identity in teachers' future oriented discourse. *Teaching and Teacher Education*, 24(7), 1935–1946. https://doi.org/10.1016/j.tate.2008.04.008

Van Manen, M. (1977). Linking ways of knowing within ways of being practical. *Curriculum Inquiry*, 6, 205–228. https://doi.org/10.1080/03626784.1977.11075533

Van Manen, M. (1991). Reflectivity and the pedagogical moment: The normativity of pedagogical thinking and acting. *Journal of Curriculum Studies*, 23, 507–536. https://doi.org/10.1080/0022027910230602

Valli, L. (1997). Listening to other voices: A description of teacher reflection in the United States. *Peabody Journal of Education*, 72(1), 67–88. https://doi.org/10.1207/s15327930pje7201_4

Wallace, M. (1996). Structured reflection: The role of the professional project in training ESL teachers. In D. Freeman and Jack C. Richards (eds.), *Teacher learning in language teaching* (pp. 281–294). New York: Cambridge University Press.

Walsh, S., & Mann, S. (2015). Doing reflective practice: A data-led way forward. *ELT Journal*, 69(4), 1–12. https://doi.org/10.1093/elt/ccv018

Wassermann, S. (1993). *Getting down to cases: Learning to teach with case studies*. New York: Teachers College.

Wright, A. (2010). Second language teacher education: Review of recent research on practice. *Language Teaching*, 43(3), 259–296. https://doi.org/10.1017/S0261444810000030

Xu, H. (2015). The development of teacher autonomy in collaborative lesson preparation: A multiple-case study of EFL teachers in China. *System*, 52, 139–148. https://doi.org/10.1016/j.system.2015.05.007

Yang, S. (2009). Using blogs to enhance critical reflection and community of practice. *Educational Technology & Society*, 12(2), 11–21.

Zahorik, J. A. (1986). Acquiring teaching skills. *Journal of Teacher Education*, 37(2), 21–25. https://doi.org/10.1177/002248718603700204

Zaid, M. A. (1995). Semantic mapping in communicative language teaching. *English Teaching Forum*, 33, 6–11.

Zeichner, K. (1983). Alternative paradigms of teacher education. *Journal of Teacher Education*, 34, 3–9. https://doi.org/10.1177/002248718303400302

Zeichner, K. M., & Liston, D. P. (1996/2014 [2nd Edition]). *Reflective teaching: An introduction*. New Jersey: Lawrence Erlbaum.

Index

CPSIA information can be obtained
at www.ICGtesting.com
Printed in the USA
BVHW042344160819
556031BV00006B/15/P

9 781781 796535